ADVANCE PRAISE

"At the AICCCA, we equip organizations and agencies to help consumers manage their debt and to educate them about making sound
financial decisions. It will likely come as no surprise that car financing contributes to substantial amounts of debt for many Americans.
A consumer advocate in the making, Ragsdale's intriguing and educational new book exposes an industry that for too long has been taking
advantage of those who support it with their hard-earned money."

— DAVID C. JONES
President, Association of Independent Consumer
Credit Counseling Agencies

"Mark Ragsdale possesses in-depth knowledge of the inner workings
of the automobile business acquired during his many years as a dealer,
trade association leader, and from direct dealings with top-level OEM
executives . . . He is eminently qualified to comment on and advise people
inside and outside our industry about how processes and policies may
be improved. His book, *Car Wreck*, identifies the systemic dysfunction
in parts of our industry, and explores how things may be improved."

— ALEX LARKIN
Manager of National Franchise Development at Mitsubishi Motors
North America; Former Manager of National Dealer Development at
Kia Motors America; Former National Dealer Development Manager at
American Suzuki Motor Corporation; Former National Dealer Planning
and Placement Manager at Hyundai Motor America

"It's a fascinating read on how the financial wise guys in the auto industry, as in the real estate field, have all but destroyed our economy along
with what used to be our leading industry. Very interesting and compre-
hensible analysis of how the economics of buying, leasing, and trade-ins
actually work from the dealer's standpoint—vital info to car buyers."

— RICHARD GOODKIN, ESQ.

"Mark Ragsdale's great book is the first I have read that has been written by somebody who has lived rather than observed the dealer business. He offers a clear and fresh perspective, which shows how the interdependency of the industry really impacts the consumer. Mark's book should be read by anyone in the industry. More importantly, it is a 'must-read' for anyone about to enter a dealer showroom."

— IAN BEAVIS
Executive Vice President, Nielsen IAG Automotive Group

"In his new book, Mark Ragsdale calls car dealers the 'Forgotten Man' in today's economy. The reality is, dealers are often just as frustrated by automakers as consumers are. Mark provides an honest look at what has befallen this industry, the role dealers have played, and what both dealers and consumers can do to reform it. *Car Wreck* is a great look at a massive industry and all of the different entities—dealers, banks, car companies, consumers, etc.—who play a role in keeping it afloat."

— BILL FLINKOW
Former 20 Group Director, National Automobile Dealers Association

"At MS Auto Retail, we strive to provide solutions and technologies that will enhance the businesses of car dealers. And while our solutions are some of the most innovative out there, Mark Ragsdale proves with *Car Wreck* that sometimes some good old-fashioned experience-based advice can also do the trick."

— JOHN REED
Director, Automotive Retail Solutions, Microsoft Corp.

"As Mark so clearly discusses, the relationships in every area [of] the automotive industry are clearly broken ... The relationship between the manufacturer, the dealer, the financial institution, and the consumer are all at risk ... I believe that this book may provide the impetus to start multiple conversations that hopefully will ultimately repair the relationships ... It is an easy and very interesting read and could easily become a part of both the retail and wholesale training programs."

— DON PEARCE
Former Vice President of Service at Kia Motors America; Former Vice President of Parts and Service at American Isuzu Motors Inc.; Thirty-Year Automotive Operations Executive

Car Wreck

Car Wreck

How You Got Rear-Ended, Run Over, & Crushed
by the U.S. Auto Industry

MARK RAGSDALE

LANGDON
STREET
PRESS

ISBN-13: 978-1-934938-65-2
ISBN-10: 1-934938-65-3
Library of Congress Control Number: 2010920143

Publisher's Cataloging-In-Publication Data
(Prepared by The Donohue Group, Inc.)

Ragsdale, Mark.
    Car wreck : how you got rear-ended, run over, & crushed by the U.S. auto industry / Mark Ragsdale.
        p. ; cm.
    Includes bibliographical references and index.
    ISBN: 978-1-934938-65-2
        1. Automobile industry and trade—United States. 2. Automobiles—Purchasing—United States. 3. Selling—Automobiles—United States. 4. Loans, Personal—United States. 5. Automobile dealers—United States. I. Title.
    HD9710.U52 R34   2009
    338.476292/0973   2009943109

*I Dedicate This Book In Loving Memory of
Donna Hileman, Bernie "Fred" McGrath,
and the Wonderful Families they have Blessed the World
with, despite their Untimely Departure:
Especially Wayne & Jake Hileman and
Marypat & Emma McGrath.*

CONTENTS

FOREWORD

The U.S. auto industry is experiencing the biggest crisis of our lifetimes, undoubtedly the worst in the history of the business. It has experienced the lowest sales in 30 years, some seven million fewer vehicles manufactured and sold this year than the pace it enjoyed just 24 months ago. Both Chrysler and GM, two of the nation's Big Three, have received government bailout money and emerged from Chapter 11 bankruptcy. The automotive supplier base is teetering on collapse. The federal government is now in the auto manufacturing business, the finance business, the insurance business, and the customer rebate business. Nationwide manufacturing plant, vendor, supplier, and dealership closings have cost hundreds of thousands of American jobs. Chaos reigns!

Many of the U.S. auto industry's problems are the result of its complexity. Each of its elements, from manufacturing to marketing to bank finance to sales, is interwoven with and codependent on the others. Consequently, as the industry has declined, we've seen that if just one of those elements is struggling, the problems ripple throughout the entire industry. To take an example from reality: If banks are suffering from a credit crunch, then they can't lend money. If banks can't lend money, then consumers can't get financing. And if consumers can't get financing, dealerships can't sell cars. The entire industry is dependent on things working exactly the way they should—and yet they never do.

In response to this crisis, today we are seeing a massive transformation in the auto industry. Some changes are intended to keep the industry afloat in anticipation of a better economic climate. Others are meant to help the industry blaze an environmentally responsible path into the future. There is turmoil and transformation happening at every level and in every aspect of the industry. *Car Wreck* couldn't have come at a better time, as the media broadcasts coverage of auto industry happenings almost daily. In his book, Mark Ragsdale provides a critique and analysis of those issues, touching upon all aspects of the industry—dealerships, banks, marketing, automakers, unions, and government.

Mark is a former multi-franchise, multi-location car dealer. His experiences in that arena have deeply influenced the information he provides in this book. In it, he furnishes consumers with advice on how to better navigate the car-buying process—from a dealer's perspective. He explains how finance companies and banks operate— from a dealer's perspective. He provides commentary on the fate of the auto industry—from a dealer's perspective. And for good measure, he throws in some political and government commentary from—you guessed it—a car dealer's perspective.

While industry insiders and dealers alike are sure to find *Car Wreck* a great read, the true beneficiaries of Mark's work will be consumers themselves. I am talking about those hardworking Americans, who every few years face the process of buying a car. For them, this book provides insight they won't likely get anywhere else—an insider's look and secret decoder ring—revealing what they will face as they walk through the showroom or service-lane doors of a dealership. In *Car Wreck*, they'll find a valuable guide to help them through this process.

For those of us in the industry, *Car Wreck* provides a challenge. I've known Mark for 10 years. He is an interesting, intelligent, entrepreneurial, opinionated, and captivating guy. I have dealt with thousands of dealers as the Executive Vice President of Car Business for Volvo North America and as President and CEO of Kia Motors America. While many of them remain my friends to this day, Mark stands out for his raw intelligence and unbridled passion. I caringly describe him as someone who is "vociferously disgusted with the world, yet still loves life."

While I have no quarrel with *Car Wreck's* factual accuracy, I don't agree with *everything* in the pages of this book. If you're a professional working in the industry today, I suspect you won't either. As I've said, Mark comes from a dealership background, and that background clearly influences the opinions, information, analysis, and frustrations he shares with us all.

While I don't agree with everything Mark has to say, or at times, the tone he uses to criticize the industry, there are some areas where he hits the nail squarely on the head. For example, he expertly describes the interrelationships between dealership sales, bank/manufacturer financing, and car manufacturers as codependent business relationships that are often riddled with envy, distrust, and misunderstanding.

Regardless of whether you and I agree or disagree with all or some of Mark's message, one thing remains true: *Car Wreck* provides an important dialogue at a critical time for the auto industry. With it, Mark has opened the doors for industry professionals to challenge his opinions by providing *their* side of the story and *their* vision for the future. Will it differ from the view of the future Mark lays out at the end of the book? Probably. However, with a little compromise and good decisionmaking, I think everyone—consumers, automakers, dealerships, and banks—can find a comfortable meeting ground. *Car Wreck* just might be the first step in that direction.

—Peter Butterfield
President and CEO, ATK North America, Inc.
Chairman, Lakefront Capital Partners
Former President and CEO of Kia Motors America
Former Executive Vice President of Car Business
for Volvo North America

PROLOGUE

*"We're in a giant car heading towards
a brick wall and everyone's arguing
over where they're going to sit."*
—Dr. David Suzuki Ph.D.
Geneticist, Environmentalist,
Broadcaster & Author

How do you like your new car?"

An unexpected voice interrupted Jill's daydream. She was taken aback, unaware of a friend standing behind her in the grocery store checkout line.

"We like it a lot," Jill replied. "Sometimes I have to remind Jack it's *my* vehicle though. Who can blame him? He's stuck driving my old Civic."

"You guys traded in his Mustang, didn't you?"

"Yeah, a lot of good it did us," Jill snapped sarcastically. "We didn't even get what we owed on it. *And* the ad we saw on TV was just a bunch of baloney. We ended up paying almost $100 more per month than we planned."

"New cars are so expensive," retorted her friend, attempting to ease Jill's obvious and lingering frustration.

"That's the thing. We didn't even get a *new* car! We had to settle for a used one . . . I think they call it a program car, or something like that."

"Wow! It sounds like you *did* get ripped off. A hundred bucks more per month and you still ended up with a *used* car? Didn't you bring your dad along to help with the negotiations?"

"Yes. We were there for over three hours. Jack and Dad tortured everyone in the showroom, including our salesperson. But looking back on it, I really don't understand how that whole business works. They seem nice enough. But I think we got the short end of the stick. Thank God we won't have to go through it again—at least for a few more years."

Jill is not alone. For much of the last half-century, frustration toward the car business lived no farther away than your office water cooler, local pub, or Sunday barbecue. If you ever questioned the driving forces behind the anguish of car buying, read on. If you were ever curious about the real goings-on behind the guarded walls of the automobile industry, read on. If you work somewhere in the automobile industry; from the assembly line, to the dealership delivery lane, or in the banking industry underwriting all this madness—read on.

Not only will you be better equipped to protect your wallet as a consumer, but I will also make you the resident auto industry expert within your circle of friends. While others postulate and theorize, you will know the inside story behind the industry: why it is currently failing and how it can be fixed. Think of this book as your *secret decoder ring* into a subject everyone guesses about but few truly understand.

I know you're angry. I helped make you that way. I was a car dealer for twelve years owning six franchised auto dealerships and three franchised motorcycle stores. I have been banging around dealerships since the age of seven. And I am going to teach you all the things you'd never know about the car business by telling you all the things I shouldn't.

The stuff you would never see on TV news. A fair warning is in order though. What I have to say may anger you even more.

I am a messenger of truth, but no angel. I consummated car deals I knew in my heart were not in the best interest of my customers, deals I would not have made if I were sitting on their side of the table. I was neither their clergyman, nor their financial advisor, but a car dealer trying to score as big a profit possible. Profit is not a four-letter word. However, nothing I ever did, or any other dealer might legally do, could rival the rear-ending you are taking by not knowing what you don't know.

There are dozens of books that can guide you on how to negotiate your best *price* at a car dealership. I hope they are helpful to you. Negotiating with professional negotiators can be a scary endeavor. Manufacturers, banks, unions and the government love when a new one of these consumer guides hits the shelves. It keeps them out of the limelight. As you chase after an extra thousand dollars or so in savings at the dealership level, these institutions manipulate the market value of your trade-in, keep you in debt, reduce your credit rating, and altogether prevent you from driving what you would otherwise be able to afford. They operate with little or no oversight; flying under the radar, using the public face of car dealers to hide their indiscretions.

There are reasons why you owe more on the vehicle you drive than it is worth. There are reasons why your car payment goes up each time you trade for an essentially equivalent model. One thing I know for sure, dealer profit is not the cause. You have far *bigger* fish to fry than purchasing your next car or truck at dealer cost. I say this with absolute assuredness, regardless of your personal wealth, income, debt, or credit situation. No matter who you are, I'm talking to you.

I lived and participated in the mistakes car dealers continue to make in this business, so I refuse to let them off the hook. However, only by exposing and confronting the true rule makers—the players formerly shielded from your view and sheltered from your scrutiny— can we fix the industry. As I expose and offer solutions to those that destroy your finances, lend you money, sell you cars, and wreck the industry as a whole; some folks are going to be angry with me. I expect this book to raise a few eyebrows and downright embarrass people.

Fixing much of this stuff, as well as, protecting your self-interests, requires arming yourself with the inside truth. Opinions provided by someone sitting in a boardroom or behind a news bureau desk no longer count. Shell games and perpetuated misconceptions have no room here. I have nothing to lose.

Most folks assume car companies, dealers, and banks conspire to relieve you of your money. Nothing could be further from the truth. We are too busy cutting each others' throats to stomach one another. In order to implement the revolution I offer up in this book, every player—including you the consumer—must alter his course. I leave no room for prurient short-term agendas. There is no time for that. The industry has commanded $63 billion in taxpayer bailouts. A government task force has nuked some 2,000 car dealerships off the map, with thousands more to follow. Dealers' businesses continue to be confiscated, closed, and handed over to more favored candidates. Unholy, unethical, and immoral alliances between unions, the federal government, and car companies trample our laws under foot. The casualties of their unfettered actions include thousands of otherwise profitable businesses now forced into bankruptcy! Apparently they are *not* "too big to fail," in the eyes of our politicians.

Nearly 250,000 displaced dealership workers are losing their jobs directly as a result of the government using your tax money. Might your industry, your individual small business, or your job be next?

Despite trouncing our Constitution in the name of the common good, the government continues to throw your tax money down a bottomless pit; without remotely identifying the changes necessary for an industry turnaround. Newsflash: Green Technology and CAFE standards may feed a worthy ecological agenda. UAW (United Auto Workers) ownership of the car companies may feed a worthy ideological agenda. But neither fixes the auto industry or our economy. I will explain why.

Dealers are solely responsible for delivering all the automobiles ever to be built in this country. They do so, while being maligned by extreme bias in the American pop culture. They endure the latest whims of their automakers' management, while stroking adulterous relationships with fickle, fair-weather bankers. They navigate senseless legislation that gains votes for bill sponsors, but hinders commerce and hobbles the economy. These Trojan horse laws are designed to look pretty enough on the outside. But they serve as nothing more than smoke screens hiding the real issues—those that rear-end you, run you over, and crush you the quickest.

Yet dealers are nowhere on the list of anyone's priorities. Other than those who feed their families by working at dealerships, they are not even on the radar screen. Dealers are *The Forgotten Man* in our economy. Consequently, an industry that has survived two world wars, four recessions, an economic depression, an energy crisis, and periods of double-digit inflation; now faces the prospect of building and selling some seven million less automobiles this year than it did just two years ago. As the federal government attempts to plan our economy as if it were an elementary school lunch menu, we find ourselves on the wrong track. The pain train has just left the station, filled with the least scrutinized mishandling of taxpayer money in history.

But before you break out a box of tissues (or your wallet for another round of car buying), I need to teach you about this business: why dealers, banks and automakers behave the way they do, how the rear-ending you have taken wrecked the entire industry, and what must be done to fix the whole mess.

Government-appointed Auto Industry Task Force Whiz Kids take note. You may learn something.

One

The Car Salesman's Language: Why They Keep Using It

...Even Though You Hate It

"Language is the source of misunderstandings."

—ANTOINE DE SAINT-EXUPERY
Aviator & Writer (1900 –1944)

Jack and Jill Hill wed two years ago. Jack would have married her straight out of school, but Jill wanted to wait until they had purchased their own home. So they gathered a collective $12,000 in savings, borrowed another $5,000 from her parents, and settled on a small colonial in a great neighborhood. This was the recommendation from various Internet blogs Jill had consulted while performing the couple's due diligence.

She was a pragmatist. Jack admired this in her. His impulsive nature, on the other hand, allowed a couple of credit card balances to get ahead of him. He usually made just the minimum payments, but not always on time.

The Hills arrived at the dealership in Jack's Mustang. Oh, how he loved that car! He'd graduated technical college, landed an apprenticeship, got an apartment, and finally bought his boyhood dream buggy. *Two years new and too bad it had to go,* he thought. Their first baby would be here in just six short months. They needed something else—a reliable mommy-mobile—one that didn't leave Jill feeling old and farty.

Jill liked the idea of driving a Crossover. She found it appealing that technology could now fuse a sport utility vehicle (SUV) body with a passenger car frame. They didn't have to contemplate the potential social censure of owning an actual SUV or worry so much about fuel economy. Best of all, Jill wouldn't have to drive one of those ugly family vans—like some of her friends did—looking and probably feeling much older than a young mom should. She wasn't planning to cut her hair short, either.

The TV ad showing the Crossover traveling through desert and snow and on past several gas stations, made the vehicle look great. The $21,935 "starting" price appeared affordable, but after running it through her Excel payment calculator at the special 60 month factory rate of 1.9%, the payments were still too high. $385 per month was nearly the same as they were paying on the Mustang. With the baby coming and Jill taking leave from her job, their payments needed to be under $300.

And there it was. ABC Motors' cable TV ad; "No Money Down and Just $269 per month!" So she loaded Jack into the second love of his life and off they went to the dealership. Maybe they could get the payments even lower by trading in the Mustang, she thought.

Jack and Jill were expecting the $269 they saw on TV. Of course they didn't take in the details in the ad, because they were on screen for just five of the advertisement's total thirty seconds. They paid no attention anyway, distracted instead by arguments over *Jeopardy* answers. And even if the Hills had read all the fine print, would they have been able to prequalify themselves for the offer? Unlikely. It would be almost impossible for consumers to qualify themselves with all the gibberish disclaimers at the end of ads.

Their salesperson, Eric, and the dealership he works for, are blessed by the opportunity of the Hills' visit today. However, they are also cursed with the challenge of revealing the truth to them. They must disclose the facts about the ad for which the Hills probably won't qualify and the dreaded reality about Jack's Mustang. Nobody from the dealership had yet appraised the car or asked them what they still owed on it. But the couple's ability to trade cars today looked entirely grim in Eric's eyes. So he self-governed his hopes of selling the couple a car today, deciding instead to remain hopeful.

The Hills had a plan: a clear agenda that customers prepare, prior to ever stepping foot in a car dealership: Get in. Get information. Get out! Their playbook read like John Madden's advice on my son's PS3 NFL Football video game. Hone the product-shopping list. Herd up some information. Then hightail it out of there as expediently as possible, careful to avoid any decision-making environment where pressure may loom.

Car dealers, on the other hand, make a living out of putting customers into a decision-making position.

No Decision = No Income = No Dealership.

The canyon between these conflicting agendas creates a whole lot of friction in dealership showrooms. Amidst this almost cartoonish sheepdog-versus-coyote routine, the ensuing discord yields *only* one sale out of every five customers visiting ABC Motors. This 20% "closing" ratio remains the industry average. Not to say that four out of five customers buy nothing at all. Rather, most buy something from another dealership, becoming the one in five tallied by competing dealers.

So the retail side of the industry has developed its own language to slow you down and sell you a car. This language delays the delivery of bad news until everything is written down and put out on the table. It is devised to keep you from getting angry or discouraged before you have selected a vehicle. The whole program is designed so you won't storm out the showroom door into the arms of a competitor. It's high time you learn this language. And you won't find it on any Rosetta Stone CD.[1]

Habla, Sprechen, Speak: Showroom Language

Prior to stepping foot onto the dealership lot, Jack had folded up the couple's unwritten game plan and tucked it inside the pocket of his Rambo suit; the figurative armor he had donned for their impending car shopping battle. Otherwise perfectly nice people morph into stealthy, well-heeled combatants when visiting a car dealership—a self-defense mechanism designed to retard purchase decisions. He'd also secured the help of Jill's dad, who would provide reinforcements by joining them later on at "Battlefield Dealer World."

Ironically, salespeople find themselves more intimidated by customers than the inverse, as is so commonly assumed and reported. Eric feared Rambo might be the only customer he'd see all day. Salespeople anticipate their sales manager's scorn as they explain why their customer, Rambo or not, has "walked" without buying. Any sales manager worth his salary demands an introduction to *all* customers, whether they are buying or not. Salespeople fear these unsuccessful encounters will affect their closing ratio, subjecting them to further censure and possible job loss. So they often decide not to report a showroom guest to management if things don't go right during the first minute or two of interaction.

Eric presumed, from twenty paces away, that the couple was looking to trade the Mustang. His brown belt in paranoia kicked in. His inner monologue chattered away: What did they owe on the Mustang? How would his sales manager value it? I think he just wholesaled one like it at the auction and lost money! After all, what could a rear-wheel-drive sports car be worth in October, with the snow season coming and all? I wonder what their credit is like? Here comes Rambo . . .

None of his thoughts registered on his face.

"Hi. Welcome to ABC Motors, my name is Eric." He was a decent-looking young man, a year out of community college, his hand extended for a shake.

Eric knew that customers like the Hills tend to recite the same limited number of questions and proclamations when they first meet a salesperson. (The following excerpts are listed with many thanks to Grant Cardone's training manuals. Grant is a leading industry trainer who has revolutionized salesperson language in thousands of dealerships nationwide.)[2]

1. "What's your best price on that _____ over there?"
2. "What will you give me for my _____?"
3. "What are your interest rates?"
4. "I'm going to three dealers today and the lowest price gets my business."
5. "I've been to XYZ and got a price on this _____. Can you beat it?"
6. "I've only got 10 minutes."
7. "I'm just gathering some information for my _____ today."
8. "I am just looking today!"
9. "I don't want or need any help. Can I have your business card?"
10. "I don't need the runaround. Can I see the manager to just get the best price?"
11. "How much do you require down?"
12. "Do you have any _____ in *lime green* with a *zebra* interior?"
13. "I saw one of these _____'s for thousands less!"

Eric had suffered through countless hours of dealership training and role-playing with his management team and fellow salespeople on this material. Over and over again they'd practice customer point-of-contact drills. The dealer insisted on spending a tremendous amount of time and money on this training. Sometimes he would even send in phony shoppers armed with video cameras in their handbags to test, record and replay the salespeoples' public performance.

But at the end of the day, Eric knew making a deal came down to isolating and addressing a customer's expectations—as unreasonable as they may be. Before either Jack or Jill even opened their mouths, Eric knew two pieces of information: the couple had an unrealistic payment budget in mind, and the Mustang, at a minimum, was going to be a major problem.

Eric grappled with the Hills' requests, refusing to do battle with Jack's Rambo alter ego. He needed them to drive the Crossover, get their Mustang appraised, and sit down at a desk, to receive (and hopefully) accept a deal proposal. If Eric handled it right, his odds of selling a car more than doubled. He could raise his closing ratio from 20%, to more than 50%, by staying on track and out of conflict. He had learned these truisms from his boss during many company trainings.

Once a month, the dealer would hold a Saturday breakfast meeting at a local hotel. Every employee from each of his five dealerships would attend in order to recognize the company's top performers. Sales, service, parts and office personnel who excelled at their job would receive gift certificates, cash awards, jewelry and trophies. The meeting lasted about 90 minutes, including breakfast, with a lot of movement between topics and award winners. The dealer made announcements of new performance contests and challenges, available only to those who attended the meeting. Absenteeism was a no-go for go-getters.

The last ten or fifteen minutes of each monthly session was reserved for the dealer's motivational speech. At these times, he would preach that most car deals are made or lost by failing to either *surrender* or *comply* with the customer's wishes. "Tell them 'No Problem!' Then write it down in front of them, so they know you're paying attention. By the time they leave, you will have given them all that information," he'd rant. "You need to get the customer down on paper. You've got to get them to the "write-up.""

The write-up is the time when the dealership could formally present its offer to a customer. The dealer had tracked the results of those visitors sitting down and receiving numbers, versus those who did not. Liars figure, but figures don't lie. Salespeople such as Eric were more than twice as effective in making a sale by reaching this point. Eric had learned it was essential to avoid conflict, at all costs. This strategy holds especially true with the likes of Rambo!

Eric had prepared and practiced all the answers to Jack's borderline badgering ahead of time. But it proved to be only half the battle. He confined himself to asking only powerful questions and steering clear of weak ones like the plague. These are the queries customers like Jack and Jill Hill hate and impede Eric's potential sale. Interrogatories such as "How much do you want to pay per month? How much money do you have down? How much do you expect for your trade?" These not only cause every salesperson in every dealership in America to sound like the same broken LP record, but they invite customers to lie.

Customers fear overpaying for vehicles in the most profound way. When they hear this language, they assume the worst: A greedy salesperson or dealer is attempting to max out every opportunity to make more money on them. So they lie. "I have no cash to put down. I can only afford two hundred dollars per month." Answers such as these provide salespeople with nothing more than useless, negative data anyway. Even more harmful than the resulting damage to a salesperson's attitude, is the emotional place it brings the customer. The answers they give, create holes customers will not be able to climb out of, thanks to their principle or pride. If a salesperson asks the wrong question and the customer sticks to his guns—you have a dead deal.

Basic sixth-grade math castrates these questions further. Eric knows the bank balance the couple still owes on their Mustang may cost $200 per month by itself. If he could just add that $200 to the $269 advertised payment they saw on TV, he might have a deal. Quote them a $469 payment in the first five minutes of conversation however, and Eric would see the Hills storm out of the dealership as quickly as they came in.

No. For the time being Jack and Jill were unaware of such troubles. And Eric wasn't about to bring the topic up until they were seated at his desk, with a written deal proposal for them to sign. This strategy doubled Eric's chance of selling a car. Instead, here are the questions Eric asked. "What can I get you information on today? Did you buy that Mustang new, used or as a demonstrator? When is your next payment due? How much is it? How did you get your payment so low? Who did you finance it with? How have they treated you?" Collection of such innocuous-sounding data gave Eric all the information he needed to *go pass go* with a minimum amount of sustained brain damage to he or his customers.

You see, Eric understood and appreciated the Hills' strategy and agenda. He wanted to accommodate the "gather information quickly" part on which he and the Hills agreed. However, Eric needed to gather information *from* Jack and Jill, delaying delivery of the information they came seeking. Why? Simply put, most customers cannot buy what they want. Let me repeat that, because it is important. *Most customers lack the financial ability to select, purchase, and take delivery of their primary choice of vehicle.* Why? There are just too many personal, technical impediments in order to make all the pieces of the deal fit together.

The auto industry plays a game of averages, where dealers attempt to put issues within the ballpark—the smaller the ballpark, the better. In three out of four car deals, the pieces have to be fit together like one of my daughter's jigsaw puzzles. So that's the game dealers play; sitting in the bleachers with a nine-year-old girl's Jumbo Puzzle.

The pieces include the customer's personal credit, his income situation, and the fact he just plain owes too much money on his trade-in. Most car deals require working with a combination of all three, in order to gain loan approval from a lender. These factors juggle the amount banks will advance or loan on a particular new car, how much is still owed on the old one being traded, and any other income or credit baggage each customer is carrying. Seventy-five percent of the time dealers must arrange financing around these issues in order to deliver a car.

No Solutions = No Financing = No Deliveries = No Dealership.

None of this has anything to do with satisfying either the customer's primary choice of vehicle, or the monthly payments he expects from advertising. Blindly showing the customer his primary choice of vehicle can be—and usually is—a big mistake. If personal obstacles crop up too late in the negotiations, they can prevent the customer from buying his first choice. Even worse, this usually embarrasses him or her out of purchasing *anything* from the dealership altogether. I refer to this as "the champagne taste on a beer wallet syndrome." Once customers taste champagne, beer doesn't go down quite so easily. And hard feelings are caused by a salesperson denying customers what they feel they "rightfully" deserve. More deals are lost over consumer egos than money in this country. And frankly, most if it is avoidable if salespeople, their managers, and dealers, would remember this one simple fact.

I cannot tell you how many times customers came into my Chevrolet dealership looking for a brand new Tahoe, got the information, left to "think about it," and later took delivery of a much less expensive SUV or used Tahoe from the competition. We had an opportunity to offer the lower priced model to these customers *before* we ever presented the much larger Tahoe figures, but we didn't. Why? We were afraid of the customer's potential negative reaction and began making decisions for him, rather than offering all his alternatives up front. Essentially, we chickened out, practically handing the deal and our customer, to the competition.

It is true that some customers may have hit the lottery and can buy anything they want from the dealership. Perhaps even the dealership itself if they so desire! However, these situations are old-school anomalies. The farmer with stacks of moldy mattress money stuffed into his overalls sometimes shows up in dealership folklore. In reality, the dapper-dressed dandies face the same financial challenges as folks in torn jeans or Adidas track suits. I have chided the salespeople I have trained throughout my career with the words of Grant Cardone: "You go ahead and make a living off all the lottery winners. I will take everybody else. At the end of the year, let's see who has sold more cars and made more money."

That's the whole language game in a nutshell. The dealer's plan is to delay talking about ads for which you may not qualify. He will put off explaining why your trade-in is not worth as much as you expect or even still owe on it. He will try to place you in a closing situation, when everything is down on paper, when the issues can be isolated and addressed. Nonetheless, potential car deals still blow up every day in showrooms across America, as evidenced by the industry's cruddy closing ratio. On average, dealerships only deliver one out of every five customers.

CHAPTER

Two

Why You Will Never Get "Enough" for Your Trade-in
... No Matter What You Paid for It

"A highly popular or desirable car with limited availability will depreciate more slowly than a car that is in sufficient supply or less desirable."

—CHARLIE VOGELHEIM
Vice President, Auto Development,
J.D. Power & Associates

Let me discuss the single-most-prevalent issue the auto industry faces today; the one Eric is about to experience with Jack Hill and his Mustang. Most Americans drive cars worth far less than the principal and interest penalty amounts they owe their banks. Those vehicles involved in an unrecovered theft, or "totaled" in an accident are troublesome to car owners' finances and credit. The sizable disparity between what consumers owe their banks and the much lower market value covered by their insurance company is a perpetual liability to most folks. This is known as the gap—the difference between what one owes on a car and what it is worth.

Special gap insurance is available to cover these differences, but few buyers purchase these policies from their dealers. One really good thief or really bad accident later, and the insurance company only funds part of the loan payoff. Consumers are on the hook for the rest. I am not talking about shortfalls ranging in the mere hundreds of dollars. I am talking thousands. The terms used by the industry to describe this phenomenon are; negative equity and upside-down. Most everyone with an existing auto loan is upside-down today. In February 2009, Edmunds.com reported that the average consumer's negative equity was $4,700.[3] In 2005, Edmunds reported the average at $3,500.

I've personally seen these differences range from a few thousand dollars to well over $10,000. I once worked for Dana Goodfield, Massachusetts State Automobile Dealers Association (MSADA) Past-President. A recent customer visiting his Chevrolet-Volkswagen dealership tried to trade a Dodge Neon with an Actual Cash Value (ACV) of $4,500. Meaning, similar Neons were selling for this same approximate amount at auction. No problem. Except the customer still owed $19,500 on it! Meaning he "owned" $15,000 in negative equity, or was $15,000 upside-down.

TABLE 1:   **A Real Example of Negative Equity**

	$19,500	Owed on Dodge Neon
-	$4,500	Neon's Actual Cash Value (ACV)
=	**$15,000**	**"Negative Equity" or "Upside Down"**

When someone is this upside-down, dealers refer to the customer as being "buried." Well, get out a backhoe, because this one is deep! You see, one could buy a brand new Neon, put no money down, and still not owe even $14,000 on it. But this guy owed $19,500 on a car that didn't sell for that much brand new! Situations of this magnitude occur when customers "roll" their growing negative equity problems into successive new loans again and again, instead of making them up in cash each time they trade. Most customers have perpetuated this cycle the last two or three times they've traded a car. Some even more.

Negative equity is without a doubt the single most prevalent issue in the market today. The second is consumers' revolving debt, or credit card balances, and the third is overall consumer credit scores (now driven by the housing crisis), in that order. We will never and I mean in my sincerest Massachusetts accent, *neh-vah* solve the last two problems without remedying the first.

While watching the legislative hearings and key player interviews regarding the Big Three bailouts, I was vexed by how little attention was paid to this epidemic. Automobile negative equity continues to spread faster than a sneeze on a commercial jet. It cannot be solved by simply negotiating a better deal or purchase price at the dealership. Consumers buying below dealer cost still get nailed. It cannot be solved by some automaker Employee Pricing strategy so in vogue with the domestics. Rebates make the situation even worse, as you will come to see. To the automobile market and the industry as a whole, negative equity is the macro-financial equivalent to H1N1 Influenza. And Congress is off mixing up the wrong vaccine.

Here is a classic example of a customer in this situation. I could not have done a better job painting this picture if I made the story up myself. With guilt I admit, despite the financial misery involved, it makes me chuckle. If it weren't so serious, it might be funny. Therefore, I believe I have aptly named her "Jane Dough," and placed my personal remarks in parentheses:

"I currently have an '06 Isuzu Ascender that is in good condition. Kelly Blue Book values it at $16,550. I know I won't get that exact amount . . . but I am hoping to get close to that as I can. I would like to get an '07 or '08 Toyota Camry LE or Honda Accord LX or EX. I don't have a lot of cash to put down right now—maybe $500. (Which won't even cover the sales tax and registration fees and thus—isn't really a down payment at all) *I have poor credit, although we bought a house a little over 7 months ago.* (A loan no doubt cosigned by taxpayers such as you and me via Fannie Mae and Freddie Mac) *So far, there have been six payments due and we have made every payment on time.* (Like this is an accomplishment?) *Also, we have two cars—my husband's is*

in his name only and mine is in both of our names with him as the primary borrower. We have never been over 30 days late with those either. (Another accomplishment? Newsflash: Making payments on time is not an accomplishment. Rather, it is an obligation.) . . . *I tried to trade the SUV in at an Acura dealership about 5 months ago, but they turned me down because they said I am too upside-down. Currently the 10-day payoff is $21,803 and the 20-day payoff is $21,909."*

Many thanks to the anonymous *Yahoo Answers* contributor for this 2007 story and to the gentleman who answered in this way; *"It doesn't seem like a very good move to trade in for several reasons . . . My suggestion . . . is to wait a year at least before getting a new car. Swallow your pride and just accept the car you have for the time being."* (I couldn't have said it better myself). [4] By the way, the answer-man purported himself to be a "banker".

What the automakers, government, and surprisingly the media miss, is the commonality of Jane Dough's situation throughout the consumer marketplace. Throwing money at automakers, so they (or the UAW) can live another day to build another car that most people could not buy even if they wanted to, denies the real problem. Jane's story is neither an anomaly nor an aberration. She represents the norm.

The term being upside-down was formerly reserved for dealers and their sales staffs. Today, customers commonly inject these words into the first minute of their showroom conversation, particularly if they have received an education from a competing dealership. Usually these angry refugees need some confirmation they are in such bad shape. They often get it by cross-shopping one competing dealer against another, due to frustration over treatment deemed unfair. Most customers assume dealer greed is the culprit. This is surely the case some of the time. However, competition has a way of flushing out greed, provided there are enough competing dealers still operating in a given marketplace to keep each other honest.

Despite; "I never get enough for my trade," being the mantra of today's buying public, most folks' focus and attention is elsewhere in the transaction. They look for the big discounts, with resentment or flat-out refusal in paying "sticker" price (Manufacturer's Suggested Retail Price or MSRP) for a new vehicle. Feeling this provides too much profit for the dealer, they typically arm themselves with dealer cost information and Rambo suits. However, no matter how much they study and master negotiating skills to rival a Moroccan Bazaar, most everybody still gets nailed with depreciation the moment they register their new vehicle. My buyers often openly leveraged this fact while engaged in price negotiations, without having any idea why.

You Are Your Own Worst Enemy

"I'm going to lose thousands on this brand new car the minute I drive it off the lot."

"You are right, Mr. Customer. Why don't you let me show you how to lease this new one, or purchase a used one?"

"No way. I want to *own* my car, not lease it. And I don't want to inherit somebody else's used car problems. So let's just get down to negotiating a better deal and I'll buy it."

No Problem. Who was I to argue? I made a living selling cars, not winning arguments.

In truth, the *initial* shot of depreciation is due to neither the quality of a vehicle, nor the dealer's profit motive. It is in fact, almost entirely due to the attitude of consumers themselves, that is, the difference in price consumers demand when buying a *nearly* new car versus a *brand* new car.

For example, if I offered you a current model year used vehicle with 1,000 miles on it for $1,000 less than a new one, would you buy it? No? My customers usually wouldn't either. It would often require $3,000 to $5,000 or more in savings, in order to cajole a buyer into purchasing a nearly new used car instead of a brand new one. The most common customer-cited reason for this perceived value disparity; "I don't want to inherit somebody else's problems."

Obviously dealers attempting to resell a now used car to a market that demands large discounts can only pay (or offer in trade) so much for that car. Otherwise, the dealership would take a loss when reselling it. If customers were readily available to buy nearly new cars for somewhere close to the value of a new one, cars would initially depreciate far less.

So who is really causing this huge initial depreciation loss the customer hates so much? The market is. And who makes up the market? You, your cousin, your uncle, your neighbor, and your co-worker; to name a few. Dealers cannot give you more for your car than someone else is willing to pay for it. And somewhere in the middle the dealership must make a profit. Customers seem to be regularly disappointed in their dealers and do not get this basic reality. The very same customers who are happy to scoop up huge discounts on current model year used cars, later curse their dealers if the shoe is on the other foot and they are trading one back in. Of course, this is not being very accountable from the customer side of things, is it? Can I get an *Amen* from Dr. Phil?

J.D. Power Initial Quality Survey

Besides the customer's complicity in this initial depreciation issue, there are other contributing factors to overall depreciation. Most factory folks (and some consumers) tend to be very centered on J.D. Power & Associates' Initial Quality Survey. J.D. Power is a company that conducts customer satisfaction research on new car quality and long-term dependability. Its Initial Quality Study (IQS) is a measure of problems experienced within the first 90 days of ownership, or more specifically, the number of failures per 100 vehicles produced.[5] For example, the economy car segment averages roughly 135 defect failures per 100 cars produced. Therefore, if two friends bought a Model X subcompact at the same time, they would experience roughly three component failures combined between the two cars.

Consumers doing research on initial quality may consider one vehicle over another based upon these studies. However, Power's IQS only measures the first 90 days of vehicle operation and is not a real predictor of the depreciation beating consumers often take. On the other hand, dependability—especially at the sixty or seventy thousand-mile mark—aggravates depreciation at virtually any age or mileage. Vehicles having a reputation for falling apart farther on down the road simply do not attract many used car buyers. Fewer buyers mean lower prices.

While the industry has made leaps and bounds with short-term quality, the long-term dependability improvements aren't quite so pretty. This number is only improving by roughly 5% per year.[6] Since domestic cars have a less than stellar quality reputation in their past, they have fallen down the ladder in the viewpoint of our pop culture. That slip makes their products less desirable. Those Sunday afternoon cookout stories have an impact. You've either participated in, or overheard, the conversations I am talking about: Somebody's bellyaching about their Escort, while a Honda Civic owner beams with 100,000-mile reports of trouble-free ownership! People listen.

Domestics, as well as even the Korean manufacturers who had such early quality problems, have figured out how to compete in IQS. But reputations are hard to change. Factories can't rebuild the cars they've already manufactured and need to live with the black eyes they have earned by building inadequate products in the past. The J.D. Power IQS measures the here and now and is published for everyone to see.

Initial quality-focused consumers build product shopping lists and more importantly, justify their purchase decisions to friends and colleagues around such numbers. Everyone wants to be seen as a prudent buyer. Most folks want their purchase choices to be judged by onlookers as in vogue. Consequently, automakers focus heavily upon IQS. Also, they often pay a lot of money for Power's consulting services. I attended Kia Dealer Advisory Board meetings where he was engaged to give an opinion on one of Kia's initiatives. I sat next to him. He is an extremely intelligent and articulate man. Thank God, because he has a lot of influence over automakers, which influences the choices we all get to make as consumers in the future.

However, at least with respect to controlling vehicle depreciation, the longer-term survey is far more relevant. I know the manufacturers have some of this data. I have seen the estimates Kia had compiled prior to extending their new vehicle warranty term to ten years/ 100,000 miles. So at least some of them know what will go wrong with their vehicles over the long term. Manufacturers need to focus on fixing those things on the assembly line *now*, before the cars are driven seventy or eighty thousand miles, start costing their owners money, and get dumped on at cookouts—regardless of what J.D. Power's IQS says.

Meanwhile, despite consumer paradigms regarding the right price to pay for a nearly new car and manufacturers prioritizing the proper industry surveys, folks owe thousands more on their vehicles than what they are worth. There are several more substantial pieces of the puzzle causing this to "happen". I put "happen" in those quotation marks because this is not a freak accident of nature. Instead, it is the result of an institutionalized double dipping of consumers. You get double-dipped by the automakers, the unions and the banks. Let's start with the automakers who design, price, and market the cars we drive.

Three

How Rebates and Rental Cars Cost You Money

... More Than You Could Ever Imagine

*"There is nothing so useless as doing efficiently
that which should not be done at all."*

—PETER F. DRUCKER
Writer (1909–2005)

Some vehicles today have but $600 in factory-to-dealer markup. Kia's new Forte model, built as a replacement for their Spectra model, has just $550 in total markup between dealer cost and MSRP. I have sold the Chevrolet import-fighting Aveo model, which provided less than $400 in total profit before expenses to the dealership. Who cares right? You should. Why? Because if you spend all your time negotiating discounts off of those kind of numbers, you are setting yourself up for the financial penalty of the rest of the story. What is the rest of the story? Read on.

How many consumers have purchased a new vehicle on Monday, then found out the rebates went up on the following Saturday? I have seen a particular product's rebates go up or down as much as $7,500 in that short time. I've delivered vehicles in that scenario, when customers lost money by being a little too early or late buying their new car. Of course, there was no way either the customer or I could predict whether factory incentives would go up or down, because that information is kept secret by automakers. The only information released by manufacturers is the current incentives available and an end date to the program. Consequently, consumers play Russian roulette when buying rebated products—most vehicles on the market today.

Rebates are used by automakers to cajole customers into purchasing cars off dealer lots, or so they purport. In reality, rebates are used as a mechanism to structure car loans—a practice you will come to understand. Structured and approved car loans sell cars, which, believe it or not, manufacturers care little about. Why? Because dealers have already bought and paid for those cars. The factory's job is essentially done! However, a potential and often perpetual problem remains: As cars sit unsold at dealerships, dealers stop reordering them, causing unsold product pileups for factories.

The alpha and omega behind any rebate program is to help dealers move product off their lots, so they reorder inventory from the manufacturer. That's it in a nutshell. Miss the timing of these rebates as a consumer, though, and you overpay by thousands.

But the fun doesn't stop there. Every customer in the country who has purchased the model now being rebated finds himself having paid too much. Not only the consumers who bought current model year vehicles are affected. "A receding tide lowers all boats," in the words of President John F. Kennedy. This means if the price of the new ones go down by $7,500, for example, the value of one, two and three-year-old models depreciate that much faster as well. Since most vehicles are currently financed, customers' loans also go further upside-down as a result of the current rebates.

Did Jack Hill concern himself with current Mustang rebates when considering trading the car? Of course not. Like most consumers, this issue is off Jack's radar screen. But it is on ABC Motors' radar screen! New vehicle rebate increases and decreases immediately affect used car auction values. If, for example, the rebate on Model X goes up by $3,000, then every brand new Model X can now be purchased for $3,000 less. Because consumers demand similar price savings on all the used models just like it, dealers begin buying and trading used Model Xs for that much less as well. If you are among those trading in a used Model X during this time period, you lose out along with the rest of the market. Rebates cost you money.

Having already purchased, traded, and stocked similar used models prior to the rebate-driven price reductions, dealers are regularly clobbered by those cars in their inventory. After all, they cannot sell them at auction without taking a loss due to the now lower post-rebate market values. Dealers suffer a multiplier effect of negative equity across their used vehicle inventory in this way. In a real sense, every time a dealer buys or trades for a used car, he risks rebates and other market factors depreciating the vehicle before he can sell it. The used car business is riskier than playing the stock market.

As a Cadillac dealer, I became very aggressive with selling used Sedan Devilles. I quickly learned to be careful with how many I carried at any one time however. The values of those vehicles fluctuated as much as $2,000 per week at auction. I dragged my wife to a sale in New York, where I disposed of some overage Sevilles, STSs, an Eldorado, and an Allante, which remained unsold in my used vehicle inventory. I lost $32,000 on eight cars that day. She was not impressed. I was more focused on the ten retail used vehicle sales I would have to deliver, in order to make up for that huge loss.

These kind of hits are not specially reserved for Cadillac dealers like me. Manufacturers across the board adjust rebate values with consistent unpredictability. Dealers stock these different brands on their used car lots in order to offer customers a decent selection. As a result, a dealer's used car inventory is a constantly churning depreciation dumping ground where all the collective rebates on the market take their deflationary toll at the same time. Dealers go upside-down to a much greater degree than is possible with any one individual customer, because they have so much inventory depreciating at the same time.

The term dealers use to describe the situation is under water, or, water in their used car lot. Water in the inventory is the total loss of value between what dealers paid for their used car inventory, at time of purchase, or trade, and what they would all sell for at auction today. It is not unusual to see dealers and the banks that finance their inventories (called floorplan loans, as you will come to know) go under water by as much as six figures at times. My personal record while operating five stores simultaneously was a half-million dollars! I have had a single store's used vehicle inventory tip upside-down by as much as $250,000; the equivalent of six months of hard-earned net profit.

Rebates cost both dealers and their customers serious money. They also hammer automaker margins because the cash rebate incentive programs come directly off their bottom line. They really are bad for everyone in the industry; building, buying, selling, trading, or financing cars.

Ironically, while rebates serve as the major mechanism by which cars and customers lose equity, banks make the situation even worse. Lenders use rebates to bury current negative equity problems into new loans. This means if a given customer is several thousand dollars upside-down in his trade, banks utilize rebates on the new car to make the new loans "look" better. How? Lenders set auto loan limits based in part on the *original* invoice price of a vehicle, regardless of whatever rebates are subsequently made available by the manufacturer. Lenders use these incentives to cover up their customers' negative equity problems by allowing them to effectively borrow the total invoice price *plus* the rebates, in order to pay off their old car loan.

This really doesn't solve customers' upside-down condition at all; it just monkeys with the numbers in order to write new loans and sell more cars. Of course, this puts the consumer in an awful position. Owing the bank several thousand dollars more than the vehicle can be purchased for makes him several thousand dollars upside-down right from the start. Shell games such as these just delay consumer pain, allowing lenders to charge more interest and turn the customer successively *more* upside-down each time he trades cars.

The good news: The scheme has allowed impatient consumers to get what they want, when they want it, regardless of the financial consequences. The can gets kicked farther and farther down the road each trade-in time, until the end of road is reached. This is when there is no way to get the finance transaction anywhere close to the original factory invoice. There simply are not enough rebates to play the game anymore. Those customers reaching this point get stuck; forced to keep their cars just like Jane Dough.

Do you feel like an auto industry crash-test dummy in all this? Do you feel rear-ended? Good. There's more. As voracious as rebates are in eating up your finances, rental cars hurt you even more. Not the fact that you can rent yourself a ride when you travel, but what rental cars do to the value of the one at home in your driveway.

The Devastating Effect of Rental Cars

"Fleet game" is the term I use to depict the wild deals manufacturers make with rental car companies such as Hertz, Avis, National and Enterprise. Such programs entice these players to buy cars in tremendous volume. Volume deals move a bunch of units off the factory's back with the stroke of a pen. Automakers heavily subsidize these volume price offerings via enormous fleet rebates. These incentives virtually eclipse any normal rebates designed to motivate retail customers and their banks.

Fleet cars are billed through a "chosen" dealership, which customarily receives a $50 per unit profit before expenses. Many times, the cars never touch the delivering dealer's lot. Rather, they are drop-shipped directly to the rental company. In this way, automakers use licensed dealers—which are necessary under law—but pay only a pittance for the service. During the late 1990s, I delivered nearly 100 Pontiac Grand Ams to Enterprise Rent-A-Car under this system, in two separate transactions.

We have already talked about the market depreciation issues inherent with customer rebates. However, the real damage in the fleet game comes *after* automakers repurchase or buy back the used rental cars from the rental companies. That's right. The automaker guarantees to repurchase those cars from the rental company when they hit a certain age or mileage.

The time and mileage of repurchase customarily occurs within the current model year of the vehicle. This means that 2009 product is both sold as new and repurchased used within the 2009 model year. The plan allows the rental companies to project their cost of ownership during the time they will be renting these vehicles to their customers. Automakers actually offer you this type of protection when you choose to lease rather than buy your car. More on this later.

Once the manufacturer repurchases these cars from the rental companies, it liquidates them en masse at dealer auctions. Dealers purchase the auction vehicles at staggering discounts below original invoice cost and then offer them for sale to customers, on their lots, at a profit. Some of these fleet auction sales feature hundreds of current year or one-year-old, low-mileage vehicles in the same day; one after the next, after the next . . . The color selection is limited, but the supply is so enormous, the prices plummet uncontrollably. Every Tom, Dick and Harry dealer in the market has his nit pickiest choice of bumper-blemish disqualifications. Final bids are settled within $50 differences.

And when all the dealers have had their fill and the cars have been auctioned for next to nothing, dealers compete against a bundle of the same Tom, Dick, and Harrys, all over their market, selling the *exact* same used cars.

Far more importantly to you is the hammering your trade-in value takes as a result of this glut of cars and their liquidation value prices. You can lose close to half your money buying one of these models new, the instant it is registered. When I say "lose half your money," I mean; if you finance the whole purchase and your car instantly becomes worth half of what you financed, you immediately owe the bank double what the car is now worth.

Similarly, yet far more drastically than with customer rebates, is the way in which this flood of cars devalues two and three-year-old models as well. These lower market values trickle down quickly—massively deflating the value of similar models of all ages. Just as with customer rebates, dealer and bank inventory equity positions go under water literally overnight.

The worst case of this I've ever witnessed was the 2006 Ford Taurus. Original sticker price was around $22,000 on dealer lots. Ford provided a sweetheart deal to the rental companies, bought the cars back from them, as per their contracted schedule, and sold them by the thousands at dealer auctions. At the time, a dealer could buy one of these $22,000 beauties with 12,000 miles on it for around $10,000 at auction.

In a vanishing act, all the equity of all the Ford Taurus customers disappeared. All those buyers taking delivery of a brand new one that year and the year before and the year before that got rear-ended! No matter what they paid for their new Taurus—no matter what kind of fantastic deal they negotiated with the Ford dealer—*the price turned out to be too much*! No dealer discount or aggressive trade-in policy could ever rival this kind of financial beating.

But the Mac Daddy move on how to "make you really upside-down" comes, once again, from the banks and their convoluted loan guidelines. Same stuff, different day in making new upside-down loans look better. They based their used Taurus loan limits around new Taurus invoice prices. This allowed them to advance up to $19,000 on each, from the car's introduction in September 2005, through April 2007. After that, the NADA (National Automobile Dealers' Association) guides began publishing 2006 used vehicle loan value averages and the jig was up.

In the meantime, dealers (like me) and our customers had a field day with these "program" cars, scooped up at auctions for fifty cents on the dollar. Dealers could buy a Taurus for $10,000, mark it up $2,000 in profit and still save the customer somewhere around $10,000 over a new one. So far, so good. However, the real damage to consumers occurred when they took advantage of the banks' liberal lending guidelines, rolling in up to $7,000 worth of negative equity. In this way, folks financed $19,000 on a $10,000 car. All this with no money down!

TABLE 2:   **Fleet Game Financing of Negative Equity /
           Making Your Situation Worse**

	$10,000	Dealer Cost on Taurus (Market Wholesale Value)
+	$2,000	Dealer Profit
+	$7,000	Old Negative Equity Rolled In
=	$19,000	Financed on $10,000 Car
=	$9,000	**New Negative Equity (Upside Down) Position**

The wholesale market value of a 2006 Taurus was set at just $10,000, because that is what they were selling for at auction. If you were trading a 2006 Taurus at the time, you would receive no more than $10,000 for it. So all the customers were actually receiving in value was $10,000. But customers were able to finance up to $19,000 and did so, in order to re-bury their current $7,000 negative equity problems, into the newer Taurus loans. Financing $19,000 on a $10,000 car is preposterous. Loaning that money for six, seven or eight years—insane! But that's what we did.

At the end of the new transaction, our customers were even further upside-down. Instead of carrying just $7,000 in negative equity on their old vehicle, they found themselves instantly $9,000 upside-down on their newer Taurus'.

$19,000 financed - $10,000 value = $9,000 upside-down.

Most automakers play the fleet game. Most auto lenders use similar invoice-based loan guidelines, despite the substantially depressed values that fleet cars bring to the party. However, neither Toyota nor Honda has succumbed to the temptations of rental car sales or consumer cash rebate wars. At least not to any substantial degree. Consequently, these two automakers command some of the highest resale values in the industry. This translates into far less depreciation, less negative equity, and less customer anger at trade-in time.

This has nothing to do with the superior quality of the cars they build, either real or perceived. Anyone that tells you Honda and Toyota hold better resale values exclusively due to building better vehicles, doesn't fully understand the economics of the car industry. Why do I mention this? Governmental closings of up to 42 percent of GM and 25 percent of Chrysler dealerships leave these failing automakers little choice but to rely upon fleet games to move product in the future.

Fleet games are a big part of what put these car companies in the shape they are in today. Ipso facto; the government doesn't fully understand the economics of the car industry. Yet they hold the keys to these companies as well as the keys to the future of thousands of dealerships who might otherwise keep fleet games off the automakers' menu.

Why Automakers Play Fleet Games

Aside from quick volume sales orders, one might wonder why automakers would ever choose fleet game tactics. Folks at the factory know these strategies ruin their product's resale value. So why do they do it?

In today's world, automakers sell cars to rental companies and rebate their products—heavily at times—in order to keep union shifts working. Shift stoppages incur substantial UAW contract penalties, including up to two and a half years of wages payable to laid-off workers. It's an either/or proposition: either they pay laid-off workers to stay at home or they continue building, discounting, and rebating cars that nobody wants. And you, the consumer, pick up the tab in the form of accelerated vehicle depreciation. In a very real way, consumers are paying for this union entitlement, also known as jobs banks.

On February 10, 2009, Ford Motor Company announced it had negotiated jobs banks penalties out of its UAW contract. Ford's decision to reject federal bailout money in 2008, coupled with threatening the UAW with bankruptcy, forced the union to come to the table. In traditional bankruptcies, union contracts are virtually worthless to the courts. They most surely would have been ripped up and thrown in the wastebasket by a judge, forcing the UAW to work under whichever conditions the bankruptcy court mandated. So they acquiesced, getting rid of the jobs bank clause that they most assuredly would have lost in bankruptcy court anyway.

In the cases of GM and Chrysler, however, the UAW leveraged the federal bailout money, its relationship to the Obama administration, and, jobs banks clauses as tools to gain ownership of the companies. This occurred via a very non-traditional, government-structured bankruptcy.

In the meantime, the jobs banks clause has hammered your resale value. Moreover, jobs banks opened the door for your tax money to buy GM and Chrysler for the union; a benefit they were not entitled to under bankruptcy. We all got rear-ended by this clause. All except the UAW of course.

Here is House Speaker Nancy Pelosi's position on the unions and automakers: "I don't see how unions are an excuse for automakers not to innovate." With all due respect to the office, innovation is not even on the radar screen in solving today's auto industry problems. Ecological innovations are legislative and executive branch constructs and agendas. They are not the reason the industry is faltering today. Negative equity, trickle down job losses, and overall consumer credit take that prize. The role the UAW plays is far more relevant. Its actions necessitate rebates and fleet sales, resulting in the financial hammering consumers suffer today.

Professional Democrats don't want to hear this because the unions represent a major piece of their constituency. Ironically, consumer protection is a major piece of the Democratic Party's agenda as well. They can't have it both ways though. Either fleet games cause depreciation or they do not. Either consumers are negatively affected by depreciation or they are not. Politicians cannot ingratiate unions and protect consumers at the same time. At least not in this case.

Every time automakers heavily rebate a car or buy one back from the rental companies for mass auction disposal, they affect consumers like Jack and Jill Hill. They affect the value of the Mustang the couple is trading in as well as both the unpaid balance and future value of the Crossover the Hills are trying to buy. Unions are a major reason why automakers and the entire industry now find themselves in this predicament. And as a reward, they own a giant chunk of it today. It's like giving a kid who burned down a school the deed to the property.

While used car buyers, cookout stories, rebates, and rental cars are depreciating the vehicle you purchase and drive; the federal government and two-thirds of our state governments permit auto lenders the most predatory interest rate calculation method imaginable. By either act or omission, the politics behind this double-dipping is astounding. Our lending system has found a way to charge you interest twice; once on the principal balance you borrow and once on the excess depreciation of your automobile. The same government that preaches consumer protection through a series of do-nothing auto industry regulations, has allowed this rear-ending. Let me explain.

CHAPTER

Four

How Banks Charge You Interest, Penalties, & Interest on Penalties

... *Crushing Consumers with More Debt than They Bargained for*

"It is well enough that people of the nation do not understand our banking and monetary system, for if they did, I believe there would be a revolution before tomorrow morning."

—HENRY FORD
Founder of Ford Motor Co. & Innovator of
Assembly-Line Manufacturing (1863–1947)

Many consumer auto loans are formulated via the Rule of 78s.[7] Huh, I hear you say? First, I need to give you a couple of definitions. Principal is the amount of money you borrow in a given loan. If you take out a loan for $10,000, your principal balance is $10,000. Interest is the extra money you have to pay back to the bank on top of the principal they loaned to you. Interest is the bank's profit in loaning you the money.

Now, let me give you the definition of the Rule of 78s: The total number of months' interest due in a 12-month year equals "78." Simply put, on the 1st month of the loan, there are 12 months of interest due. On the 2nd month of the loan, there are 11 months of interest due. And so on and so forth up to month 12, when only 1 month of interest is due: 12 + 11 + 10 + 9 + 8 + 7 + 6 + 5 + 4 + 3 + 2 + 1 = "78."

That's it! This explains why they call it what they call it. However, I still have to show you how the rule works, and more importantly, why it hurts you.

The following article excerpts are taken, with thanks, from the website of Pine Grove Software, Princeton, New Jersey.[8] My insertions are noted in parenthesis.

> "Outside of banking circles, the Rule of 78s is little understood, even though it is commonly applied to many consumer and business loans (like auto loans). For the borrower (you), it tends to have an insidious effect in the nature of a hidden prepayment penalty . . .
>
> The theory of the Rule of 78s is that at the moment a borrower signs the Note, then he is immediately obligated to pay back all of the principal and all of the interest that will accrue in the future over the agreed term of the loan.
>
> Now, if the borrower prepays, the lender "generously" forgives some of the interest even though this additional interest has not been earned (by the bank). Lenders argue that the uncertainty created about an early payoff entitles them to some compensation for being at the borrower's whim. (Banks consider it a whim if you prepay the loan early and this applies to every time you trade in a vehicle on which you still owe money!)
>
> Two general rules of thumb:
>
> 1. The higher the interest rate, the greater the penalty amount.
> 2. The earlier the prepayment in relation to the term, the greater the penalty amount.
>
> So if you're a lender, you should love using the Rule of 78s. If you're a borrower, you should try to avoid it (like a social disease). Let me give a caution for lenders: Some states have usury laws and others limit use of the Rule of 78s.[9]

In 1992 the federal government outlawed the use of the Rule of 78's on loans exceeding sixty months (five years) in length. In 2001, federal legislation was introduced to eradicate its use altogether. The proposal died in subcommittee. Seventeen states have outlawed the rule's use, overall. Thirty-three states, however, still permit the practice up to the federal limit of sixty months.

In those states still allowing use of the rule, essentially the practice of "usury" is legalized. How? Banks levy interest penalties against consumers attempting to pay off their loans early, later adding those penalties onto the consumer's next car loan. This scheme effectively charges consumers interest on top of interest, double dipping them in a practice also known as usury.

Take a quick look at the rule of 78s as it applies to a $5,000, 12-month loan, calculated at 5% APR. The days of 12-month auto loans really went by the wayside in the 1950s:

TABLE 3:   **The Rule of 78s on a 12-Month Loan**

Month	Payment	Interest	Principal	Principal Payoff	Interest Penalty	Payoff After Penalties
1	$428	$21	$407	$4,593	$135	$4,727
2	$428	$19	$409	$4,184	$131	$4,315
3	$428	$17	$411	$3,773	$126	$3,899
4	$428	$16	$412	$3,361	$119	$3,480
5	$428	$14	$414	$2,947	$110	$3,057
6	$428	$12	$416	$2,531	$100	$2,631
7	$428	$11	$417	$2,114	$87	$2,201
8	$428	$9	$419	$1,694	$73	$1,768
9	$428	$7	$421	$1,273	$58	$1,331
10	$428	$5	$423	$851	$40	$891
11	$428	$4	$425	$426	$21	$447
12	$428	$2	$426	$0	$0	$0
Totals	$5,136	$136	$5,000			

Now look at *today's* average car loan: $20,000, 60 months, calcu-
lated at 7.9% APR, using the Rule of 78s. You will note the interest
penalties are far more onerous. I trimmed the lengthy table down, so
you can see where you stand every six months on a five-year loan:

TABLE 4:   **The Rule of 78s on a 60 Month (Five Year) Loan**

Month	Payment	Interest	Principal	Principal Payoff	Interest Penalty	Payoff After Penalties
1	$405	$132	$273	$19,727	$4,272	$23,999
6	$405	$123	$282	$18,335	$4,228	$22,564
12	$405	$111	$293	$16,604	$4,103	$20,707
18	$405	$99	$305	$14,803	$3,899	$18,702
24	$405	$87	$317	$12,930	$3,617	$16,546
30	$405	$74	$330	$10,981	$3,255	$14,236
36	$405	$61	$343	$8,954	$2,814	$11,769
42	$405	$47	$357	$6,846	$2,295	$9,141
48	$405	$33	$371	$4,653	$1,697	$6,350
54	$405	$18	$386	$2,373	$1,019	$3,392
60	$405	$3	$402	$0	$0	$0
Totals	$24,274	$4,274	$20,000			

In these two examples, you will notice the marked difference
between the consumer's principal payoff (the amount truly owed to
the bank at that point in time) and the much larger payoff after bank
penalties. In the sixty month loan, you can make 12 full months of
payments and still owe more than you initially borrowed!

Here is my point: Most times you take out an auto loan, you are
signing up to pay off *all* the interest that will *ever* be due on that loan.
The longer the term of the loan, the more interest due. When you pay
off the loan early, as is done every time you trade in a car on which you
are still making payments, you still owe *all* remaining interest on the
loan. Shocking, huh? Therefore, when the bank gives you your unpaid
balance over the telephone, they take all this interest due, discount it a

bit and quote you a figure that includes the unpaid principal *plus* their interest penalty.

Please note this, because it is important: *In most instances, whenever you trade in a car on which you are still making payments; this extra debt is rolled into your new car loan.* This cycle is maddening and has bilked the average car buyer out of thousands of dollars. This is further aggravated by the number of times he has paid off a loan in advance. Frequent buyers electing long-term finance contracts get buried the deepest.

The Rule of 78s is understandable from a banking perspective. Most of the bank's expenses are incurred at the outset of the loan. Most of their interest income is realized during the early stages of the loan and therefore, make the bank's profits appear larger than they are. CEOs earn bonuses on this early, often overstated profitability. In this way, the rule can be very dangerous to banks as well. Far too much principal is carried far too long into the loan. If and when a loan goes bad, the principal hasn't been reduced by much on the bank's balance sheet. So in the case of vehicle repossessions, when lenders lose money on their "repos" at auctions, banks are forced to book those losses. They can and may go insolvent at the hands of the very rule that encourages the overstated interest profits.

I saw this manifest in the theater of residential real estate loans in Orange County, CA. I decline to call them real estate "mortgages," because they compelled borrowers to pay down absolutely *no principal* whatsoever! They really weren't mortgages, but interest-only loans on houses everyone expected to appreciate in value or to become worth more over time. Everybody banked (pun intended) on staying in their house until the appreciation was adequately sufficient to justify selling it off and moving on, with a substantial profit in the borrower's pocket. We all know what happened to the value of those houses and the financial condition of the banks writing such loans. Banks booked the interest profits, took their executive bonuses, and parachuted out of town as the upside-down houses sold for huge losses in foreclosure auctions.

But cars are different beasts. Cars never appreciate, at least not before they become antiques. If mortgages on houses can get out of control, you'd better believe mortgages on cars have *no* control. Houses, if not over-appraised for finance purposes (recent catastrophe aside), either hold or gain in value. Cars, on the other hand, depreciate quickly and massively. It is bad enough to keep trading a customer every 36 or 39 months, when he has been paying primarily interest on six, seven and eight year loans. However, add to this the depreciating nature of automobiles and the whole premise proves preposterous. This is a dirty bomb going off right now in our economy!

Up until roughly halfway through the loan (three or four years of making those payments while the vehicle becomes worth less and less), the customer pays very little principal on the loan. Therefore, he still owes more on the car than its true market value. This "phenomenon" also occurred the last time he traded, becoming worse and worse, with each successive loan. Not just due to the depreciation issues covered earlier, but as a result of interest calculation methods and usury penalties.

You don't need me to tell you your payments go up substantially each time you trade in your car. Did you think those payments increased as a result of your purchasing a more expensive vehicle? Did you think dealer profit was the cause? Of course not! Most of the increase is due to the slow repayment of principal, interest penalties and the vehicle depreciation tacked onto each successive loan!

At some point these payment increases become unaffordable. But have no fear, the auto industry is here, figuring out a way to help you borrow your way out of it! The bank, the dealer, and the customer all agree to continue stretching the finance term out further towards the ends of the earth—all in the name of delaying the pain. This explains why you end up in greater and greater debt with each car you buy; a perpetuating cycle of insanity.

This has occurred repetitively, for the last twenty years in this country; growing like a boil coming to a head. And nobody talks about it: more interest charges, more depreciation, more negative equity, it all amounts to bigger problems for the customer and all the other players in the industry. This is what has brought us to where we are today. The government avoids discussing the issue like an STD. The bank lobbyists want me to zip my lips about it. And no one enables it more, copes with it more frequently, or receives more of the consumers' blame than—you guessed it—the car dealer.

When Did the Banks Sneak Up and Run You Over?

I really had to ponder why banks would keep stretching out the term of auto finance the way they have. For the last sixty years, new car prices have kept pace at somewhere between 24 and 26 weeks of average consumer salary and wages.[10] This means car prices have risen relative to wages at a constant clip since the 1950s! In the fifties however, customers paid cash or took a 12 to 24 month finance contract, often trading vehicles with their paid-off title in hand.

But banks began offering 36, 48 and 60 month financing options consecutively. Then it expanded to an unbelievable 72, 84 and 96 months! In the last ten years, the average consumer's auto finance term has increased from 52 months to 64 months.[11] Why?

At first I was tempted to believe in the "other distractions of life" argument: the rate at which everything else has increased in price. Then I realized the banks had their hands in all those cookie jars too, such as mortgages and credit cards. These were all extended-term credit items, many with escalating finance charge "gotcha" clauses. They even grab a $1.50 from every debit card transaction.

It seems banks keep moving money until the customer is at best, unsafe, or at worst, insolvent! They have made a lot of money on the auto dealers and their customers, and now most are running for the hills. They're turning their backs on the negative equity they have created in the marketplace. They have aided and abetted the crime that is our current economy, which has, in turn, created the highest unemployment numbers in 26 years. It started with upside-down home mortgages and will only end once this whole generation of upside-down car loans are addressed. People who can't work can't make car payments, so repossession rates will grow along with lenders' repossession auction losses. Banks have shot themselves in the foot too.

As repossessions grow, new auto loan approvals evaporate. Throughout my career, I have had numerous conversations with auto loan officers. They claim that otherwise approvable loans are summarily rejected due to Monday morning butt-kick meetings, held by their supervisors. As the prior week's reports of repossession auction losses come over the wire, loan buyers suffer heavy critiques and censure by their bosses. Today when trying to buy a new car, even employed customers with decent credit scores are not getting loans. This is primarily due to their negative equity situation. What do dealers do? They look for the impossible—a $10,000 car and a bank to finance $25,000 on it—at least in the case of Dana Goodfield's shopper trying to trade in his Dodge Neon!

Perhaps banks will come out with nine or ten year car mortgages soon, in order to keep customers' payments in line! In the meantime, the federal government might consider going all the way with outlawing the Rule of 78s practice. But with banking on the brink of nationalization (government ownership), that may be like asking the cat to watch the canary.

States such as Arizona, Delaware, Idaho, Iowa, Kansas, Maine, Maryland, Massachusetts, Michigan, Minnesota, Nebraska, Nevada, New Hampshire, New York, Oregon, South Dakota and Vermont have already legislated against the practice. All others have work to do. Take a look at which of your state legislators are getting campaign contributions from the banking lobby and how much. You will have a better idea why your state allows these predatory lending schemes.

Outright hypocrisy thrives in states such as; California, Louisiana, and Minnesota—where they legislatively restrict the commissions banks pay dealers to sell auto loans. Of course, its apparently okay for lenders to charge you via the Rule of 78s there. What's more, mortgage brokers and boat, RV, and farm-equipment dealers earn unlimited commissions for arranging consumer bank loans on their products. Just because pop culture places auto dealers in a different category, doesn't give states the right to act with unconstitutional bias.

Attempting to cure customer woes by regulating *dealer* profitability is like mowing your lawn one blade of grass at a time. It might make a great Trojan Horse or red herring story for the newspapers, but it does little for you. On the other hand, eliminating use of the Rule of 78s solves at least this consumer problem with one stroke of a pen.

Five

How Dealers Hide the Truth About the Car You're Trading In

... but Never Actually Owned

"Drive-in banks were established so most of the cars today could see their real owners."

—E. JOSEPH COSSMAN
Salesperson & Author

The Hills, like most consumers, had no blessed idea of all that their auto financing goals entailed beyond the basics of how much they had budgeted per month. Of course, Eric dreaded dealing with customers such as these, because divulging the realities of past decisions costs him four out of every five sales he attempts. Eric knew when he brought this dilemma to the sales manager for guidance, he would have very few new ideas how to solve the problem either. Sales managers get cranky when salesperson after salesperson brings the same story to their desk.

Eric: "I've got the Hills here. They are trading in their two-year-old Mustang and want to buy the Crossover in the ad for $269 per month. They're paying $390 per month on their car now. His credit card payments were a little shaky, but he says he always pays his auto loan and mortgage on time."

Manager: "So they want to trade a two-year-old car for a brand new car and save $120 per month in the process? Is that all?" He retorted sarcastically. "Here we go again. How much do they owe on their Mustang?"

Eric: "Twenty thousand. I offered to show them the two Crossover former rentals we have in stock, saving them around $5,000, but they want to buy new. They say they don't want to inherit someone else's problems. We really need that discount to take care of their negative equity, don't we?"

Heading back to his desk, lips loaded and armed with a buffet of payment options, Eric spied Jill's dad making a beeline toward the seated Hill couple. Eric swallowed hard. At that moment he realized Jack and Jill's reactions to the figures he was about to present were most probably superfluous. Dad was in charge.

Eric's sales manager had prepared MSRP, trade difference, an assumed down-payment figure to hit the couple with, and monthly payment estimates broken down into separate finance term lengths, all written neatly on a worksheet with a green Sharpie. The compilation of figures and ensuing presentation was, as always, structured to provide enough information to read the Hills reaction. Car dealers and their sales people call this their "initial pencil." However, depending on the drama anticipated by the size of the figures on the proposal sheet, this is sometimes referred to as the "peel them off the ceiling pencil." Because sometimes customers hit the roof.

Eric knew Jill's dad would be the one to start. So he braced himself as he laid the Hills' deal proposal onto his desk. Dad lowered his head in review. Eric recited the details his manager had given him during his lip-loading session.

"With just $2,000 cash down, your payment options are 48 months at $596, 60 months at $499, or 72 months at $439. Which works best for you?"

Dad exploded, "What the hell is this?"

Eric: "Assuming $2,000 down plus taxes and fees, I provided three payment estimates for you to choose from. Which one works best for you?"

Jack: "What happened to the $269 in the ad?"

Eric: "Well, if we extended your term to 96 months like in the ad, your payment would drop to $378, provided we could get a lender's approval." Eric turned the proposal sheet over, showing some additional options.

Jill: "Yeah, but that's still not the $269 in the ad. Plus you're asking for $2,000 cash down, which we not only don't have right now, but wasn't part of the ad price!"

Dad: "This is bulls$*t! You guys are all the same!"

Eric: "I am happy to get you the $269 ad price subject to bank approval, but you are trading in a vehicle that you owe $20,000 on. We have to pay that loan off in order to resell your Mustang. That is included in the payment."

Jack: "So? The Mustang is worth at least that much. It listed for $30,000. How much are you giving me for it?"

Eric: "We are allowing you $17,500 off MSRP."

Jack: "This *is* bulls$*t! You're trying to steal my Mustang! That's how you guys make money! You'll probably put it out on your lot and get $25,000 for it!"

Eric: "How much were you expecting for it—considering sports cars don't sell very well during the winter—and most people today can't drive stick-shifts?"

Jack: "At least what I *owe* on it! I'm not going to take a loss like that!"

Eric: "Let me get my manager, so he can explain the appraisal on your car."

Jack, Jill, and her dad are learning the same way most consumers today learn about being upside-down. Jack had traded an old clunker his uncle had given him when he bought the Mustang. He owed nothing on that wreck. He'd negotiated a decent discount and paid $27,900, almost $2,500 under sticker price. He did so by putting down $750 total cash out of his pocket—including taxes and fees—and financing the rest on a special 1.9%, 72 month rate offered by the factory at the time.

His sum total of payments after 19 months was $7,500. His principal pay-down totaled over $6,750, so Jack did a great job denting the principal balance. He achieved this feat due to the extremely low special factory interest rate. Despite not being penalized by the Rule of 78s, rebates and fleet games had taken their toll. Like most every car buyer in America today, Jack is upside-down. Savvy?

American consumers such as Jack, you, and now me, trade their vehicles approximately every 39 months, despite financing their cars for an average of 64 months. Now that you understand the problem we call being upside-down, you realize the implications. Most consumers take on new finance obligations before they have satisfied their old ones. They rarely ever truly own their car. Miss a couple of payments and borrowers will see who really owns that vehicle—the bank.

Pop culture, lifestyle changes, product endorsements, as well as advertising all help customers build a "short-list" of what they want to drive next. Except for first time buyers, the impetus to change automobiles derives from a world of perpetual personal relevance. What works today usually proves insufficient, uncomfortable or unbearable in just a few years' time. The Hills were not comfortable foraying into their impending parenthood with Jill's eight year-old, 120,000 mile Civic and Jack's winterless Mustang. They agreed the Civic had, so far, been reliable and economical, but it was not the pinnacle of safety for their growing family.

The Civic was paid off and suitable for Jack to drive. This meant the Hills could trade the Mustang and still have only one car payment each month. And that one payment was going toward a baby-ready ride. This gave them the motivation to endure the pain of tedious dealership negotiations such as these.

Sales managers and their dealers can fix the price of any car only to the limits of the discounts and incentives provided by the factory.

On the other hand, they can fudge a bit by purchasing a customer's trade-in for slightly more than market value. What they cannot do is jump into a time machine and rewrite the obligations a customer assumed the last time he signed a finance contract. Nor can they wave a magic wand and control the rate at which a car depreciates.

In Jack's case, the ACV of his Mustang was appraised at just $14,000. But when asked, Eric said $17,500, didn't he? Was he lying? No. Eric said ABC Motors was "allowing" Jack $17,500, not writing a check for that amount. Here is Jack's "trade *allowance*."

TABLE 5:   **The Difference Between "Allowance" and Your Car's True Value**

	$14,000	Mustang Actual Cash Value (ACV) or Auction Value
+	$2,000	ABC Motors Advertised Crossover Discount
+	$1,500	Manufacturer's Crossover Customer Rebate
=	**$17,500**	**Trade "Allowance" Offered By Dealer ($3,500 Overstated)**

$14,000 ACV + $2,000 in discounts + $1,500 in factory rebates
= $17,500 in trade allowance.

But since Jack would have received the $2,000 in discounts and $1,500 in rebates off the MSRP whether he traded his Mustang or not, the Mustang's actual cash value or true market value remains at just $14,000.

To explain this more simply, let's pretend the Hills are looking at a $50,000 MSRP vehicle with a $10,000 markup. This means the dealer has paid his manufacturer $40,000 for the car and the manufacturer has published and affixed a retail price label to the vehicle of $50,000. Let's further assume for illustration's sake, this fictional dealer chooses to sell his car to a relative at his wholesale cost of $40,000 (making no profit). Additionally, he is accepting a trade-in at the same time. Let's pretend the trade-in is in fact Jack's Mustang. In this case the dealer has a bunch of flexibility in how he shows the $40,000 selling price to his customer:

TABLE 6:   **Two Different Ways to "Pencil" the EXACT Same Deal**

Discount "Pencil"		Trade Allowance "Pencil"	
	$50,000 Example Vehicle M.S.R.P		$50,000 Example Vehicle M.S.R.P
-	$10,000 Dealer Discount	-	$24,000 Trade Allowance
-	$14,000 Trade-In ACV		
=	**$26,000 Cash Difference**	=	**$26,000 Cash Difference**

The customer's out of pocket money after trade-in is the same $26,000 in either case, isn't it?

Why Do Dealers Play These Games?

Dealers decide in each situation how to present the same reality. The pencil on the left side of the table above might work well for a customer who is wise to what his trade-in is truly worth in the marketplace, but is motivated by seeing a huge discount. The presentation on the right works best with customers like the Hills who "don't want to take a loss" on their trade-in. Either way, the customer's out of pocket money is identical. With a $20,000 loan payoff such as the Hills, the "loss" as customers define it remains the same in both examples.

The pencil on the right is really just a childish way of accommodating customers who are putting their heads in the sand. Oh, and banks want to see the deal this way, too. It helps them finance negative equity on deals without having to 'fess up about it. Bottom line, each customer pays the same $26,000 cash difference regardless of how the dealer shows the numbers.

However, margins like the $10,000 markup in our fictitious example are non-existent without massive dealer invoice-to-MSRP margins. Since manufacturers know customers study and compare MSRPs between competing products, they set sticker prices only as high as they dare. They then charge their dealers the maximum price possible—dangerously close to MSRP—with little discount for the dealer to play with. They want to leave as little profit possible for the dealer, opting instead to have their cake and eat it too. More of the profits, while remaining as distant from customer disappointment issues as possible. That is their dealers' job. Disastrous.

Automakers traditionally use dealers as human shields to handle the customers' financial and emotional reactions to depreciation. They do this while providing dealers with fewer tools to do the job. Invoice-to-MSRP markups have been growing slimmer with each successive model introduction. Car companies would *never* leave $10,000 markup for a dealer to play with on a $40,000 car. Consequently, dramatic charades like these are relatively non-existent today.

In this case, the best Eric and the dealership can do is show Jack a trade allowance of $17,500, making his negative equity *appear* to be $3,500 less than it actually is. Truthfully, Jack owes $20,000 on a $14,000 car! Not a good situation in which to find oneself. He is $6,000 upside-down, despite only seeing $2,500 of it on paper. ($20,000 owed versus a $17,500 allowance). Had Eric plainly explained this predicament, Jack and his father-in-law would have immediately stormed out of the dealership, with Jill in tow. So dealers like ABC Motors and salespeople like Eric all speak in terms of "allowance" rather than "actual cash value." Again, the allowance numbers game leaves the Hills with the impression they are only $2,500 upside-down while the true number is $6,000.

Might the $14,000 ACV be a *falsely* low number, designed to "steal" the trade-in and improve ABC's profit margin, as Jack alleged? Of course it could! But these shenanigans are more and more of a rarity today. Why? Because competition is fierce among same-make and competing-brand dealers. They all vie for the same customers' business in close geographic proximity to one another. The Hills could probably drive to three or four competing stores offering the exact same Crossover within half an hour's time. Leaving too much profit in a deal proposal makes easy pickings for a sharp competitor wanting to steal a customer. This is but one reason why the government's utilization of your tax money to close thousands of dealerships is a bad thing for you. What is far more common and especially in the context of fewer dealers to shop, is the possibility of a dealer's mistake in the appraisal of your trade. This is because every trade-in appraisal is nothing more than an opinion.

Every Trade Appraisal Is Nothing More Than Someone's Opinion

I first learned of this reality by attending a NADA class in Colorado Springs, CO in 1989. Our instructor tried an experiment. Every student appraised three vehicles and wrote their appraisal amount on a piece of paper, without being permitted to consult one another. Granted, many of us were from different parts of the country, with dealerships representing everything from Hyundai to Mercedes-Benz. The likelihood of us all arriving at the same market valuation on the spot was slim.

But we weren't even close. As a group, we appraised these used cars with a valuation discrepancy of fifteen-hundred to two-thousand dollars on each vehicle. I tried this same experiment myself, years later, with six managers in my own organization. They represented five of my stores at the time, all within a forty-five minute drive from one another. The results were even scarier, because we didn't have the excuse of geographic differences. Imagine, all these managers working with my customers, making or passing on deals, while commanding trusted control of my corporate checkbook. They were barely within $2,000 of each other in their appraisal of our mock trade-in! Horrifying.

Here's a prime example to support the concept that maintaining consumer choice of independently owned, same-brand dealers is vital to our free market system. My next-door neighbor, Nancy, found a $4,000 difference in trade value between two local Ford dealerships, against the same identical model, trim, color and MSRP! Not surprisingly, she got that better deal from the dealership owning the superior service reputation as well. By the way, the loser of the battle over Nancy's business shut down his store due to the economy and shrinking sales volume, at least according to the newspaper story. Either his appraising manager was napping at the time, or the winner's manager made a substantial mistake. No matter, Nancy had the choice to shop between competing dealers and benefited financially as a result.

Today, Chrysler and GM, both under government direction, are on a crusade to close some 3,500 dealerships as a means to save expenses and (allegedly) financially strengthen those whom they retain. The discarded dealers, as well as consumers like Nancy and you end up the losers in trade valuation and many other fronts.

For the purposes at hand and the "curmudgeon snipers" out there who will assert my bias in protecting ABC Motors in our story, let's assume Jack, with his father-in-law's assistance, negotiated an accurate $16,000 ACV for his Mustang. This means they will now see an additional $2,000 in allowance. I have, for example, been blessed to employ some very creative sales managers, who made deals by placing seasonally challenged trade-ins into warmer markets, like Texas. During fall and winter months in the Northeast, sports cars and convertibles can be presold or "placed" to another dealer based on a verbal description. This practice allows a more aggressive dealer to have a competitive advantage in his marketplace, by expanding his somewhat limited used car market into distant locations.

Despite all this working in Jack's financial favor, really getting some $2,000 more for the car than it was worth locally, he still managed to arrive at the point where he owes $20,000 on a $16,000 car. $4,000 upside-down is the best it will get for the Hills. At least now they are beating the Edmunds.com national average by $700.

The allowance numbers have been made to look better through discounts and rebates. This takes some of the sting out of the deal for both Eric and his customers—and more importantly—potential lenders. But the extra $4,000 is going to translate into much higher payments than the $269 ad price. Furthermore, lenders still may not loan the extra money on the Crossover to cover it. All these problems and the Hills still haven't even agreed to buy the car!

Six

All I Really Need To Know About the Car Business
. . . I Learned in High School Economics (Almost)

*"There is no such thing as absolute value
in this world. You can only estimate
what a thing is worth to you."*
—CHARLES DUDLEY WARNER
Author & Editor (1829–1900)

No matter how you package this whole mess of unnecessary depreciation, predatory interest calculations and other rear-endings soon to be covered herein; the principles governing the car business are as simple as those learned in high-school economics class. Let me give you an example:

I got my first taste of economics in a class taught by Mr. Bob Reidy during my junior year at St. John's High School. He demonstrated the principal of supply and demand by holding a doughnut auction at the beginning of each class. There were twenty-five hungry boys in the room and Mr. Reidy would bring two, four, or six various types of doughnuts to auction. The winning bidders were allowed to eat their successfully won doughnuts right there in class. Twenty-five years later, I still remember this as one of my most enjoyable and impactful learning experiences.

Mr. Reidy retained tight and exclusive control over the amount of doughnuts—the supply—in order to command asinine prices. The price per doughnut was highest on the days he brought in the fewest. In college, I learned more about this *Keynesian* economic principle. In the car business, the lessons prove to be much more expensive.

At introduction and for a short time, certain car models command stupid prices. The ZR1 Corvette, the Dodge Viper, the Shelby Mustang are good examples, and the list goes on. Customers often begrudge these margins, both real and perceived. However, dealers have a hard time benefiting from this phenomenon in any sustainable way. Why? They simply cannot get enough of a given model while they are hot, in order to affect their financial success in any significant or sustainable way. If and when dealers are blessed to get a slug of these cars and generate some game-changing volume, the demand has usually waned.

It's like Mr. Reidy allowing four or five students to hold their own doughnut auctions in class each day. There is too much competition in selling the same stuff to a limited market. When most consumers purchase their fill, supply builds up and prices erode. Bring too many doughnuts and tomorrow you will be auctioning them off as day-old pastries. In the car business, the higher the supply piles up, the lower prices must get to move the metal.

I have attended car auctions where franchised dealers brought brand new, limited edition models to the block. The most memorable was a red Dodge Viper. This particular auction was in Connecticut, so it drew dealers from a wide range of states from Pennsylvania to Maine. A few buyers who pilot their own private jets hail from even greater distances. The auction's expansive metal Butler building houses twenty active lanes. These all run simultaneously, offering everything from virtually totaled high-mileage wrecks, which sell for few dollars, to the occasional Lamborghini or Ferrari.

However, this Viper brought the auction to a virtual standstill, as dealers from every lane followed the car in to see how high it would go. The vehicle sold for twenty thousand dollars over sticker price. Now mind you, only dealers were allowed onto the grounds. So this wasn't some rogue private collector with the winning bid. This was a dealer most likely acting on behalf of a collector, or one intending to wholesale the car to another dealer (who had a collector in his pocket).

My point is this: The dealer was going to own the car for twenty grand over MSRP, mark it up, and sell it to a buyer at a profit. Today however, Chrysler and Dodge dealers are going out of business. A hundred Vipers on each of their lots could not save their dealerships. That's supply and demand at work.

There is too little profit margin in today's new vehicles for dealers to create demand. Dealers can and do create the perception of great savings, but there's not much meat behind the story without the factory's help. And this help comes via monetary incentives. The three major forms are; consumer rebates, low APR & lease offers, and factory-to-dealer cash kickbacks. These incentives arrive and depart at the pleasure of the manufacturer, designed to spur customers into buying and banks into lending. But at the end of the day, every one of these tactics must encourage dealers into making replacement orders. Otherwise it is a lose/lose scenario for the factory. They lose money on the expensive incentive and they lose out on the dealership replacement orders that generate cash.

Incentives such as these arrive with no predictability. However, as car sales slow and factory production continues, dealers count on automakers continuing to support weak sellers. In the case of General Motors, I have seen all model-line rebate programs end on a given Friday and not be replaced until the following Thursday. This happens when the manufacturers lurk around waiting for a competitor to commit to an incentive program. In this way, they attempt to match or trump each other's latest offerings.

GM has a tremendous habit of waiting to decide on its incentive programs until it sees what Ford is going to do. Meanwhile, 7,500 of its dealers are apologizing to customers about the deals they've penciled. "Now none of these figures include rebates, because those are on hold until Friday." Meaning, please don't get upset with the lousy trade allowance I just showed you and run off to buy something else just yet. I will make you a better deal on Saturday. Of course, consumers do visit competing-brand dealerships while they wait for their second pencil. And many times they do end up buying something else during the interim.

This has not led to great success with our automakers. When we were kids and played *follow the leader*, what we were really doing was submitting to someone else's leadership for a time. In this way, automakers give away and then try to reclaim market-share turf constantly. Of course, it is far more expensive to let something slip and have to buy it back, than it would have been to remain the leader. I like a quote from Henry Ford; "The competitor to be feared is one who never bothers about you at all, but goes on making his own business better all the time." In today's car companies, the financial officers set the budgets and the marketing folks get fired if the market-share falls short or the dealer reorders don't come in. Sometimes this happens because the marketing managers misallocate resources, but most of the time, finance simply doesn't appropriate sufficient funding to meet the goal.

Coming more into vogue today are incentive programs that have been prebuilt into an automaker's production plans. Kia and Hyundai for example, pay dealers volume kickbacks known as "dealer cash," based upon the number of vehicles they sell in a monthly or quarterly period. During the period from 2001 to 2004, my average profit from brand new Kia customer sales wasn't a profit at all. Before the factory kickbacks, we *lost* $500 per car—before expenses—chasing the volume necessary to collect the highest possible monthly check from Kia.

When losing money up front on so many car deals, it is imperative the store sell the required amount in order to trigger kickback payments. Missing the mark can prove financially devastating, as the losses are never restored by the manufacturer. Overall, the Koreans' strategy in this regard is brilliant. While even Japanese automakers such as Honda and Toyota are suffering sales drops in the range of thirty to thirty-five percent, Hyundai and Kia have slowed by less than six percent.

But to play this game at the retail level, a dealer must have ample cash on hand. He must pay off liens on trades while he waits for customer rebates and dealer cash kickbacks to be reimbursed by the factory. All this has become an art form in itself. I liken it to juggling with money. If you think about it, dealers actually pay automakers "retail" for their cars and "wholesale" them to customers like you. How? The dealer pays invoice, marks the car up $1,000 and sells it to a customer receiving a $3,000 rebate. In essence and reality, today's customer pays less than the dealer does for his car.

From the factory point of view, there is a very fine balancing act in the supply and demand picture. It costs "X" to sit on the cars, "Y" to get the dealer to step up and take them off their hands, and, "Z" to really get the vehicle to move in the marketplace. Decisions are *all* driven by these numbers.

The One Who Makes *All* The Decisions Owns *All* The Results

Even with all this control over supply and demand, in the end, the majority of automakers blindly blame their dealers for lack of sales. Sometimes they are right. Many times, their formula is illogical. Many factory managers are all too prepared to go find someone else to service the dealer's market if he goes under. The quickest way to go under is having too many cars on the lot!

On the rare occasions, when the stars align, dealers find the perfect storm of virtually unlimited product supply at a demand-driving price point. This is a Keynesian moment when lower prices increase volume. At such times, dealers make a lot of money by selling a lot of product at fair margins. These are glorious days, but fleeting. As soon as the factory's situation changes, so do the incentives, and the bloom falls off the rose as quickly as it blossomed.

Supply and demand are exclusively controlled by the automakers, with invoice pricing, MSRP pricing, and incentives: decisions that can and do significantly reduce or eliminate a car companies' bottom line. But the rest of the players pay an enormous price for their choices as well. All are attempting to run businesses in the absence of a stable sales-volume model. It seems like we are always looking backwards at a fire sale of incentives. And when the pressure is off, we focus on all the money we *didn't* make on what we sold. Incentives are removed and the product pile-up cycle starts all over again. Unlike Mr. Reidy's doughnuts, they are not 65¢ items that can be thrown in the wastebasket. Nobody finances a doughnut, owes too much, or trades one in for another after partially eating it.

One of the hardest things to predict in this game is when the customer is going to be ready to trade. Not when they want to trade, mind you. That happens every three years or so on average. But rather, when he is financially prepared to get a loan. Under the old model, lenders were ready for the customer when he found a newer vehicle that would carry all the debt he had built up the last few times he traded. The new model says lenders—whom we now know are running scared—are unwilling to finance negative equity.

If we could just marry the customer's loan cycle to his trade-cycle, we could count on customers being ready for a new car every few years. Remember our example tables comparing short-term loans from the 1950s to today's long-term loan nightmares? In those days, consumers arrived at the dealership with trade title in hand, truly ready to trade. Virtually any bank will finance a customer today having a fully-satisfied loan payoff under his or her belt. This makes market demand more predictable because it makes the market less reliant upon fickle banks.

Being able to predict demand accurately is tantamount to a solid industry. It would enable automobile plants to properly schedule production. That way, products don't build up on dealer lots, fleet games and incentives become unnecessary, prices are stabilized, and everyone makes money. The best part: you the consumer avoid all the depreciation losses and interest penalties you suffer today.

So far we have discussed how the system has institutionalized consumer losses through lender usury interest rate abuses, auto loan "mortgages," IQS red herrings, cookout stories, manufacturer rebates, and fleet rental car games. These issues far outweigh the impact of great versus poor purchase negotiations at the dealership. I have even shown you how to interpret the industry language that is employed to package it all up into a toxic taco—hold the tortilla—so you will continue eating it.

Now I have some good news. There is actually a way to avoid the whole mess; a way to get a new car or truck, every three years or so, at a similar payment, and never care what it will be worth at trade-in time. The average consumer and the entire industry is living in a town called Trouble, where bar-room brawls begin over vehicle depreciation and usury interest penalties. There is a stallion stabled at the local livery named Leasing. He is the right horse to ride out of Trouble. While mounted in the saddle on his back, you can either kiss negative equity goodbye or shoot it dead in its tracks.

Seven

Leasing: The Right Horse to Ride Out of Trouble

... As You Shoot Negative Equity Dead

"If it flies or floats, lease it. If it has wheels or wears red pumps, it is nothing but trouble."

—JOHN S. KRAFT
Renowned Restorer of Primitive Automobiles

So what are the potential alternatives to depreciation, long-term financing and the Rule of 78s' interest penalties? One alternative is paying cash. This gets you past the interest penalty portion, but it still leaves you the depreciation issue to contend with. Furthermore, I don't know about you, but paying cash is not a viable option for most of my family, and frankly, for most everybody I know. I have a feeling we are not alone in this regard. After looking at the U.S. consumer savings rate, I suspect automobile financing of some type or other will be necessary in order to support the industry for the foreseeable future.

Given the fact that Americans prefer to trade vehicles every 39 months, we could always go with 36 or 42-month conventional financing. This strategy avoids the interest penalties, but creates unaffordable payments. You see, even if we get 0% interest on a $20,000 car loan, when we divide the principal balance by 36 months, we arrive at a payment of $555 per month. In order for the average consumer to qualify for the loan, he would have to earn somewhere in the neighborhood of $2,700 per month *over* and *above* their current mortgage and credit card payments.

Additionally, in order to get 0% or some other low APR financing, most manufacturers' deals require consumers to forgo the rebate. This means consumers can get *either* the rebate *or* low financing but not both. You know from what you've read so far, that banks, dealers, and consumers utilize rebates to mollify negative equity in order to get new loans approved. In addition, you know that consumers' negative equity now averages $4,700 per vehicle loan. Rebates are needed to cover up this negative equity.

Since you can't get both the rebate and low financing together, manufacturer-sponsored low APR financing proves less and less viable for you to get—even though it is frequently used as an advertising hook.

Given these facts, we really must identify a solution that provides an affordable payment, can be paid off quickly, arrests negative equity once and for all, and does not involve consumers applying a windfall of cash savings. That brings us to two financial vehicles currently available in the marketplace: leasing and balloon-note financing.

Leasing strategies and details could make up an entire book in itself. Nonetheless, I am going to handle as much of it as I can with you in the length of a chapter. In order to understand how leasing works, it helps to start with the following concept: Simply *deduct* what the car is going to be worth down the road at trade-in time *from* today's cash price. How much can you deduct? That depends upon the bank or leasing company you choose. How do they make those decisions? They deduct as much as they feel comfortable with depending upon the make and model you choose. Different automakers' have different resale value track records.

When leasing a car, the customer negotiates a purchase price with the dealer just as if he or she were buying. Once the contract is signed on an agreed price, the dealer sells the car to a leasing company at that same price. This is similar to how dealerships sell conventional finance contracts to auto lenders you are now accustomed to doing business with. The leasing company (the Lessor) then leases the car to you (the Lessee) under certain terms. Those terms consist of the monthly payments you will make, how long you will make them, and the rate of interest that will apply (called a money-factor in leasing jargon).

The *Seven* Advantages To Leasing

1. You will have a much shorter term for a similar payment.

2. The impact of any cash down payments (referred to as cap-cost reductions in leasing jargon) you might make in order to lower your monthly payments virtually *double* in effectiveness.

3. In most states, you are not taxed on the entire value of a leased car, as you are on a purchased one. Rather, you are taxed on some percentage of each lease payment and/or cap-cost reduction (referred to as use tax in leasing jargon).

4. As the car is exchanged for a new one every few years, customers suffer very few maintenance or repair burdens outside of warranty.

5. There is no used car to trade in at the end of the lease term. You are free to return it, or buy it for a predetermined price at the end of the lease term if you so choose. Consequently, there is no trade payoff either. So negative equity is impossible to create.

6. On most leases you receive gap protection, guarding you from financial losses if the vehicle is totaled or involved in an unrecovered theft. This protects you from personally owing the lessor more than your insurance company covers on the vehicle.

7. The negative equity associated with your current vehicle is handled once and for all on the first lease term by some combination

of rolling it into the lease and/or putting some money down. Since it is impossible to create negative equity with a lease, at the end of your first lease term you will no longer be upside-down.

Leasing Mathematics Made Easy

Now I have highlighted the benefits of leasing, I am going to show you the simple mathematics of how it works. Let's pretend, for example, we are going to lease a $100,000 yacht. Let's say the bank estimates that in three years, the ship will be worth half of its purchase price; $50,000:

TABLE 7:   **Reducing the Amount "Financed" Through Leasing**

	$100,000	Yacht Purchase Price or "Capitalized Cost" (CAP) in Leasing Jargon
-	$50,000	Guaranteed Future Value (GFV) or "Residual Value" in Lease Jargon
=	**$50,000**	**Depreciation Expected on the Yacht**

Unlike the conventional buy financing model, where we would be making payments on the entire $100,000 plus interest, the lease calculates a payment only on $50,000 worth of depreciation plus interest. For simplicity's sake, let's assume a 0% interest rate on both sides of the comparison. I will place the yacht purchase next to the lease, so you can compare:

TABLE 8:   **Reducing the Amount "Financed" Cuts Payments in Half**

	Purchase			Lease	
	$100,000	Yacht Purchase Price		$100,000	Yacht Capitalized Cost (CAP)
-	$0	Residual Value (N/A)	-	$50,000	Residual Value
=	$100,000	Cash Difference	=	$50,000	Cash Difference
÷	36	Monthly Payments	÷	36	Monthly Payments
=	**$2,778**	**Monthly Payment**	=	**$1,389**	**Monthly Payment**

Another way to look at this is to say that in order to receive a $1,389 payment through conventional financing, we would have to double the term of our loan to 72 months, or, six long years:

TABLE 9:   **Reducing the Amount "Financed" Cuts The Term in Half**

	Purchase			Lease	
	$100,000	Yacht Purchase Price		$100,000	Yacht Capitalized Cost (CAP)
-	$0	Residual Value (N/A)	-	$50,000	Residual Value
=	$100,000	Cash Difference	=	$50,000	Cash Difference
÷	72	Monthly Term	÷	36	Monthly Term
=	$1,389	Monthly Payment	=	$1,389	Monthly Payment

And in the "buy" scenario, the resale value pressure is exclusively ours to bear. The yacht had better be worth at least $50,000 six years from now, because that is how much *more* we would have paid into it by making an extra 36 payments.

In the lease example, we are essentially pretrading the yacht ahead of time. The $50,000 Residual Value has been deducted up front, from today's selling price, affording the exact same payment for half the term. This is money we will never "owe" at the end of the lease, but rather a number around which we "own" three great options:

TABLE 10:   **Three Consumer Options at the end of the Lease Term**

Option I	Keep It!	Pay or Finance the remaining $50,000 Residual Value
Option II	Sell It!	Sell it for more than the $50,000 and Keep the Profit
Option III	Avoid a Loss!	Turn over the keys. YOU OWE NOTHING!

Many of my customers felt putting money down on a lease made little financial sense. In reality, the impact of cash down on a lease versus a finance contract literally doubles its effectiveness in lowering monthly payments; due to its shorter term:

TABLE 11:   **Doubling the Impact of Cash Down Through Leasing**

	Purchase			Lease	
	$100,000	Yacht Purchase Price		$100,000	Yacht Capitalized Cost (CAP)
-	$0	Residual Value (NA)	-	$50,000	Residual Value
=	$100,000	Cash Difference	=	$50,000	Cash Difference
-	$3,000	**Cash Down**	-	$3,000	**CAP Cost Reduction**
=	$97,000	Amount Financed	=	$47,000	Amount Financed
÷	72	Monthly Payments	÷	36	Monthly Payments
=	$1,347	Monthly Payment	=	$1,306	Monthly Payment
	$42	**Monthly Payment Reduction**		$83	**Monthly Payment Reduction**

Similarly, you can carry present negative equity into a new lease deal in the same way as a conventional finance contract. The benefit to this strategy is that all negative equity is handled during the first lease term and none of it is carried over into future deals. The entire negative equity situation is completely arrested during the very first lease term and is gone forever, unless of course, we do something unwise the next time around.

In this next scenario, I am going to get away from the yacht and go with a likely example of a car deal having an average purchase price, residual value, down payment, and negative equity figure; all at a 42-month lease term. We will keep the 0% APR interest rate for the purpose of simplicity:

TABLE 12:   **Comparison of a Financed vs. Leased Car Deal**

	Purchase			Lease	
	$22,000	Vehicle Purchase Price		$22,000	Vehicle CAP Cost
-	$0	Residual Value (N/A)	-	$10,500	Residual Value
=	$22,000	Cash Difference	=	$11,500	Cash Difference
-	$2,000	Cash Down	-	$2,000	CAP Cost Reduction
+	$4,700	Negative Equity	+	$4,700	Negative Equity
=	$24,700	Amount Financed	=	$14,200	Amount Financed
÷	72	**Monthly Payments**	÷	42	**Monthly Payments**
=	$343	**Monthly Payment**	=	$338	**Monthly Payment**

In the lease deal, you obligate yourself to 30 less monthly car payments that total an additional $10,290 for the vehicle. Does anybody really believe you are going to get $10,290 for the automobile when it turns six years old and has been driven ninety-thousand miles? Would you pay that much for a high-mileage vehicle today? No. So why would you want to gamble that anyone else might have a different opinion?

In a March 2009 comparison of the Kia Sportage 4WD LX, I looked at a sixty-month buy versus a forty-month lease, including a $2,000 down payment and $4,700 of rolled-in negative equity. In this example, the shorter-term lease was $25 per month more expensive than the five-year buy. But the extra twenty payments still made the lease less expensive in the long run. Leasing your way out of debt—this quickly—sometimes has a temporary consequence, such as, slightly higher payments during your first lease term. But your payments will never go up again as a result of carrying negative equity.

The Shorter, The Better, *Never* Sign A Long-Term Lease!

Leases of 24 months, while preferred, make the monthly cost of ditching $4,700 in negative equity substantially higher—almost $150 per month in negative equity refinancing alone. This is due to amortizing all this extra repayment over the extremely short term. After getting rid of all your negative equity in the first lease term, you will be able to better afford a two-year lease term the next go around. In the meantime, if 36 months is doable, choose that over the 42 month term. Overall, the shorter the contract term, the better it will be for you, regardless of whether you are financing conventionally or leasing. Why? You avoid all the maintenance due at the 30,000-mile mark, which on most products runs between $400 and $600. I would much rather see consumers put that money down on their next lease cycle than spend it in the service department.

I'll say it again; *if you can swing the 24-month lease, do it. You will be driving that car during the finest possible years of its life, having full warranty coverage and little maintenance.*

While running and later owning two GM dealerships and three GM brands, I had a great many customers on lease programs. Each store had roughly 350 customers on such plans. Customers would come into the dealerships prior to their first lease cycle with $2,000 in negative equity. Their options were to pay an extra $70 to $100 per month on their first lease (depending on the term chosen), or put some cash down towards it. I didn't care which. I just knew I would be seeing these customers coming back in two or three years, *not* being $2,000 upside-down anymore. In fact, they wouldn't owe anybody anything at all. What's more, if they chose a brand new version of the same exact car the next go around (second lease cycle); their payments would usually go down! This is because they no longer had any negative equity to roll into the new loan or lease whatsoever!

"But I Don't *Own* Anything at the End!"

Despite this amazing tool—and the $20,000 in training fees it cost me to learn about it—many Yankees still rebuked the program, saying the same thing you may be thinking: "But I don't own anything in the end."

To them I say: "You haven't seen the end and you never will see the end, because there is no end! Short of winning the lottery, most of us will always have a car payment. Even if you no longer pay the bank every month, you still have an implied payment. Meaning, you have a smooth, relatively cost-free ownership experience, followed by an inevitable period of costly repairs and maintenance. At the end of the day, it all averages out—one way or another—into some kind of car payment.

Folks that can't get over "I don't own anything at the end" never get to the end. Instead, they take the long-term loan, trade early, and grow deeper and deeper in debt every time they get a new car. You need to walk into your future vehicle transactions at zero: that's zero equity, zero negative equity, zero debt. Leasing provides all this. Dreaming about gaining equity through your next vehicle purchase fits the definition of insanity: doing the same thing over and over, while expecting a different result.

Those consumers still not able to get over "not owning" anything can opt for a program, similar to leasing, but which utilizes a conventional finance contract. This product is called balloon-note financing. The residual value concept is also termed differently in this case. It is referred to as a balloon payment. Unlike lease contracts, balloon-note financing compels the buyer to pay or refinance the balloon payment at the end. However, there is often a *critically important* rider contract stipulating the buyer may pay a minimal disposal fee—usually $350 or less—to get out of making the balloon payment. If there is no rider like this, don't do the deal. You will be missing out on the most substantial benefit of these products' protection against depreciation.

The bank, the automaker, and their residual insurance carriers are actually insuring the *minimum* amount your car is going to be worth two or three years down the line. Unlike with conventional financing, you really don't need to care about what that car is going to be worth at the end of 24, 36 or 42 months of lease term. With conventional financing, you essentially own all the depreciation and all the resale value risk yourself. With leasing, the other guys underwrite all that garbage.

What happens if you purchase a vehicle that ends up on NBC news as a safety hazard or is labeled by Ralph Nader as "unsafe at any speed?" No matter what you may owe the bank on that car—whether you paid cash or not—you lose precious trade-in dollars as a result. If the same thing happens while you are leasing a car, the automakers, banks, and residual value insurers take the hit. You put the *shoe on the other foot.*

Avoiding a loss is huge in today's auto market. But you even win if the vehicle's value increases over its residual value amount. If they set the residual value too low and the car is worth more at the end of the lease, you can still scoop the profit by reselling it yourself! Why take the gamble on your vehicle's depreciation, when someone else will do that essentially for free, and still leave you an upside profit potential?

Why the Government Should Encourage Leasing

American's desire to trade every 39 months coincides with the amount of time required by manufacturers to design, develop and bring a new product technologies to market. Consumers' desire to trade even more frequently will accelerate with more rapidly emerging advancements. The government wants consumers in the latest green innovations, too.

Older Technology = Lower Fuel Economy = Greater Carbon Emissions
Newer Technology = Greater Fuel Economy = Lower Carbon Emissions

Leasing fits the government's bill as well. Restoring tax credits on capital investment for banks and lease companies is a great start.

The Other Side of the Coin: Problems With Leasing

In fairness, though, there are a few challenges with leasing. In the past, automakers have put together lease plans in conjunction with lenders, that allow for attractive advertised payments. These offerings lure customers into the showroom just fine. However, banks concerned about potentially expensive repossessions and unreliable residual value estimates rarely honored the advertised specials. Instead, they typically raised their interest rates, even for customers with great credit. They also summarily denied approval of many customers having just "good" credit. This means you may have to work a bit to get a good rate on your lease. Automakers with captive finance arms such as Toyota Motor Credit, Honda Financial, Hyundai Financial and others work better than banks that do leasing as a side business.

Banks rely on residual estimates set out by an entity that publishes the Automotive Leasing Guide (ALG). These publications project the future value of brand new cars in a year, or two, or three, down the road. Calculations include deductions for excess driving and additions for certain equipment levels. This is the number banks rely upon when offering leasing programs. After all and in most cases, they will be taking this car to auction once the lease term ends. They are supposed to be able to base the whole deal on getting the car back equal to the asset amount they have reserved on their balance sheets. This allows banks to pocket the interest charges during the contract period and liquidate the car at the end of the contract, all without taking an auction loss.

Banks love leasing in principle. It gives them a lot of interest over a short contract. They actually get to charge interest on both the entire purchase price and the residual value at the same time. They are getting a "two-fer" on the interest by double-dipping on the principal, if that makes sense. As adamant as I have been in warning you about the Rule of 78s, I ask you not to worry about this particular double-dipping. It is inconsequential compared to the benefits you receive.

But if those ALG numbers are wrong on the high side, banks can get pummeled. And here is where they have trouble with leasing. If the residual value is set incorrectly, due to a miscalculation of the vehicle's depreciation schedule, banks take big auction disposal losses at the end of leases.

As you have learned, the amount that a vehicle depreciates is predicated upon a few controllable factors including: the dependability of the vehicle at higher mileage points, the supply and demand for that particular used model, and the current incentives available on brand new ones just like it. Guess who is in charge of those three factors? You guessed it, the automakers. When a bank writes leases on their best "guesstimate" of what the car is going to be worth at the end of its lease term, they need accuracy. When the factory is under pressure to move cars off dealers' lots in order to ensure dealer reorders, the bank's agenda is the furthest thing from the automakers' minds.

Therefore, manufacturers rebate the current model year vehicles, affecting the residual value of virtually every registered vehicle in the market. They sell off and repurchase gluts of backed-up models to and from rental car companies and flood the auctions with too much supply. They do everything wrong in protecting both the purchasing consumer and the leasing banks, neither of which are left unscathed by the depreciation. Instead, banks get out of leasing those manufacturers' products altogether and consumers buy alternate brands the next time around.

In managing 700 lease customers in our Chevrolet, Pontiac and Cadillac portfolios, we found 80% of these clients were renewing and picking up new cars for a second lease term. 96% were renewing for a third cycle. Even my grandparents were in on the program grabbing a new Cadillac from me every two years. Then GM blew it all up.

Cadillac Sedan Deville customers, at the outset of their first cycle, would put $2,000 down and receive a $499/24 month lease payment. By the second and third renewal we had to ask customers to pay $200 to $300 more per month—totaling $699 to $799 monthly. GM hadn't made the cars any more special to justify the increase. There were no dramatic changes to the cars.

Customers couldn't justify paying so much more at renewal time, so they bought their leased cars at the end of the term. And we went back to the same baloney of trading upside-down cars with dissatisfied customers—losing virtually all of the 700 in our portfolio. Why did GM blow away all this momentum? They simply could not fund the residual values necessary for competitive lease payments while fighting the massive depreciation caused by their fleet games. They were dumping thousands of current model year Sedan Deville rental car buy-backs at auction. The glut of cars caused the two-year-old off-lease car values to plummet along with them. GMAC (GM's lending and leasing arm) began hemorrhaging thousands of dollars on each of those lease returns at auction.

Instead of getting out of the fleet game and restoring residual values to their rightful glory, GM decided to jack customers up $300 per month at lease renewal time. Union jobs banks clauses trumped customer interests, dealer profitability and long-term market-share, in this case. Let me be clear: even in this scenario, customers were never at a disadvantage. They had all protected themselves from the reality of massive market depreciation—at least until they chose to purchase their own leased vehicles. And after doing so, they simply chose to leave. I often wonder how many hundreds of thousands of customers GM kissed goodbye because they couldn't see the forest through the trees.

In the future, it will become next to impossible to run a car company without core leasing or balloon-note financing models for consumers to choose. Production requirements are too difficult to predict, without being able to count on a quantifiable slug of customers coming back each year. Relying upon conversions and defections from competing car companies simply will not fly either.

Consumers are more and more fickle with brand selection and loyalty for sure. But the cost of advertising for them casts a costly wide net. And it is not simply a matter of running an ad folks find cute, funny, informative or inspiring. Automakers often use a methodology called the Allison-Fisher Purchase Funnel to track everything from your awareness about a particular product, to the actual purchase behavior you exhibit. I have seen Kia battle with this data for the better part of a decade—bouncing between factory and dealer responsibilities and obligations—in getting the job done. More explanation about the Allison-Fisher funnel is available at: http://marketing.gfkamerica.com/funnel/funnel.swf.

Dealers spend heaps more money to bring you into their showrooms. But just like the Rolling Stones' 1969 hit; *You Can't Always Get What You Want* . . ."if you try sometimes, you just might find, you get what you need."

Eight

How Dealer Advertising Works
... Offering What You Probably Don't Want and Can't Get Anyway

"Advertising may be described as the science of arresting the human intelligence long enough to get money from it."

—STEPHEN LEACOCK
Economist & Writer (1869–1944)

When Jack and Jill first arrived at the showroom, they were completely unaware of their upside-down issue, never mind what created the condition. They were simply armed with an ad that made certain claims; namely a $269 payment offer. Consumers such as the Hills are rarely ever able to obtain advertising offers, primarily due to negative equity and the detrimental impact it has on loan approvals. This is another of the industry's big problems: attracting customers to the showroom with enticing ads and then explaining without angering them, why they are ineligible for the offer.

More than 3,000 advertising messages inundate the average American in any given day.[12] [13] Everybody is looking for the consumer's time, attention, and money. The auto industry is no different. Car dealers spend $7.7 billion on advertising annually. Meaning, each dealership location one passes on the road, spends $365,000 on advertising every year. Every time someone buys a new vehicle from a car dealer in America today, $550 is pumped directly back into the media.[14] Automakers spend millions more researching where consumers will be, when they will be there, and whatever attention-grabbing mechanism might work. After all, their commercial is just one among the other 2,999 messages Americans endure daily.

Advertising gives the industry a frequent chance to vie for customer business in small thirty and sixty-second bites. A half-minute television spot must excite the viewer and put the product within his budget. This strategy is employed by most franchised brands and their dealers, with the exception of perhaps Mercedes-Benz and Land Rover. Their advertising is more of an exclusive message. This means they exclude a great many household budgets, which of course, makes the brand more valuable to those consumers who can afford their premium price! But most other manufacturers and their dealers are challenged with making their best financial offer while they have the viewer's attention. This leaves little time to provide all the details of the offer no one ever reads or really cares about anyway—certainly not while watching *Jeopardy* reruns. The ad is designed to tell the best truth about what is being pitched and leave the legalities to the formal contracts.

The government insists some of these legalities be included in advertisements. Television ads leave five seconds of text at the end of each spot in order to be compliant. Five seconds is certainly not enough time to explain all the intricacies contained in this book, nor should it be. Of course, what other industry besides the car business advertises monthly payments, anyway? However, dealer and some manufacturer ads do have a way of attracting legislative and regulatory attention. While the "anti-dealer advertising charge" may create great campaign fodder for a legislator or news ink for a regulator, the positive coverage from his friends at the media may prove fleeting. Scrambling to recover their piece of lost revenue from car industry ads is no easy task!

I recently watched a scenario go down in real time. Massachusetts State Attorney General Martha Coakley collected $250,000 in fines, levied against dealers, for violation of advertising statutes. The cited infractions date back to 2007. Her first dealer media target was none other than newspaper advertising. This seems ironic, given there is no five second time limit on viewing printed newspaper ads. Papers hang around a day, week or month—certainly enough time for a potential consumer to study them. In my house, our parrot poops on the ads at her cage bottom, when we are finished reading them.

Even more bizarre was Ms. Coakley's oblivion to the struggles of both the newsprint and automobile industry. A great deal of newspapers' loss of income is due to cutbacks in dealer newsprint advertising. The *Boston Globe* is reportedly bleeding a million dollars per week in operations—mostly due to cutbacks in dealer print ads—yet the Commonwealth's Top Cop focuses her energy on censuring and fining two codependent failing industries in her state.

Her attitude is a mirror of her electorate. On one end of the philosophical spectrum, the government is responsible for regulating industry—even if industry is failing—in the name of protecting consumers. On the other end, the consumer is responsible for reading their own ads and exercising personal discernment. Massachusetts voters typically support the former. Ask your local mayor, town manager, or selectman about the impact new vehicle sales and excise tax have on their budget. You will find our schools, streets, municipal buildings, and services all rely significantly upon new vehicle sales. Then ask yourself if this makes any sense.

Don't Expect Dealers to Advertise Their *Second* Best Offer

Automakers and dealers do anything they can in order to offer the lowest possible price and/or payment in their ads. Certainly, they are not in the business of publishing their second best price. This includes the assumption of an adequate customer credit rating. Credit ratings are used to secure the lowest interest rates for the longest finance term. The combination of these two critical prerequisites help keep advertised payments attractive.

Phrases after asterisks that warn; "unless you don't pay your bills," or, "only if you are acceptably upside-down," are too ridiculous to even contemplate. Requiring advertised interest rates to be placed above the lowest available in the marketplace leaves all those who would easily qualify, unfairly prejudiced.

I have a very talented dealer friend doing business in a Nevada gambling town. Most of his customers are in the service industry; supporting hotels, casinos, restaurants and retail stores. They, like most consumers today, are highly payment conscious people. From their perspective, the lower the payment, the better. My friend realizes this. So he structures his electronic advertising to convey the lowest payments possible. He has taken a position in his market as being the $88 down/$188 per month guy.

Even if he were selling vehicles at auction value, with no profit in them whatsoever, consumers electing short-term financing couldn't buy much of a car at these figures. However, by stretching the term out to 72, 84 or 96 months, consumers can get a very nice vehicle for that low payment. So that's what he advertises. When customers come in for the deal, he delivers it—so long as the banks approve the loan. What's more, he guarantees the vehicles with a huge no-questions-asked "Peace of Mind" warranty, which he has branded. Nevada doesn't require this kind of dealer warranty. He does it to be more competitive.

This kind of advertising allows the product to be placed within the budget of the intended target audience, making more customers inclined to visit the showroom. Additionally, his ads are designed to look and sound better than offers from dealers across town, who advertise the exact same product at higher payments and with no warranty. By the way, I copied much of his advertising and was successful with it in Massachusetts as well.

Since installing a pew in the showroom and praying for cash buyers does not a dealership make, dealerships often advertise their product at a loss. Of course, selling vehicles at a loss is not the name of the game. Generating showroom traffic is the point. However, eight out of ten customers shopping at a dealership end up selecting something different than the advertised car they came in on: be it equipment, color or the model itself.

Also, the dealership will be diligent with the valuation of the trade-ins of anyone interested in the "ad car." This is to ensure that every attempt is made to undervalue the trades in order to make up some or all of the loss. Eight out of ten deals involve a trade-in, making this strategy viable.

Finally, up to eight out of ten customers finance through the dealership: earning the dealer a finance commission from the lender as compensation for seating the loan. This income stream makes up some of the loss incurred by selling ad cars as well.

So based on the law of averages most dealers are unafraid of the risk associated with advertised loss leaders. Dealers who try to protect their profit margins by advertising higher prices or payments in a competitive market often underperform. They just don't see the quantity of showroom visitors necessary to close 1 in 5 customers, make money, and keep their automaker happy with adequate volume or market-share.

The most successful dealers I have seen using loss leaders offer Kia Rios, for example, at just $6,999. They do this despite the fact those ad car deals lose $3,500 apiece. But customers preferring a stick-shift, roll-up windows, and no air-conditioning—receive a phenomenal deal—irrespective of the lousy resale value of vehicles equipped this way. These dealers' stores are perpetually among the top five Kia volume retailers in the country and they make a lot of money!

They can't accomplish all this by selling ad cars though. 80% buy something else. 80% trade something in. And close to 80% finance through their dealerships. This mix along with their sales volume make their advertising and their stores highly effective.

In the case of the advertisement viewed by Jack and Jill Hill, had ABC motors used the factory programs and a $2,000 dealership discount, the Hills would have seen a $375 advertised payment. Since the Hills were working off a $300 budget, they probably wouldn't have shown up to shop the dealership. So ABC uses the factory rebate instead of the low financing and stretches out the term from 60 to 96 months (eight long years). At this rate and term, only the most stellar of credit candidates may qualify. But Bingo! $269 per month!

The Hills could have bought the Crossover for $269, but for their upside-down trade-in. Anyone else could have received the deal if they had sufficient credit. It's easy for consumers to label advertising as misleading. In many cases they are right. As they say; *unethical* advertising uses lies to deceive you. *Ethical* advertising uses the truth to mislead you. But none of it covers everyone's individual circumstances. *Caveat emptor* (buyer beware), because ads—unlike the products themselves—carry no warranty.

Nine

How Ratios and Percentages Dictate What You Can Buy
... *Whether You Like It or Not*

*"A bank is a place where they lend you
an umbrella in fair weather and ask
for it back when it begins to rain."*

—ROBERT FROST
Poet (1874–1963)

J ack and Jill Hill are still sitting at the dealership. They have decided even though they were hoping to reduce their payment to the advertised $269, their Mustang payoff made this goal unachievable. They, like most consumers, eventually concede this point by raising their payment expectations, lengthen their finance term, or throw in some cash down payment, in exchange for getting what they want. The decision was made quietly between them while Eric scurried to-and-from his and his sales manager's office to fetch an answer to one of Jill's dad's questions.

"Great news," Eric proclaimed enthusiastically as he sat back down at his desk. He was unaware of the Hills' silent concessions, but was trained to use this phrase while presenting secondary or tertiary pencils. The impact of the extra $2,000 his manager had secured for the soon-to-be-shipped-to-Texas Mustang helped his chances to make this deal. His second pencil showed the following payment options: $460 x 60 months, $405 x 72 months, $385 x 84 months.

Nonetheless he tightened a bit, unaware of the Hills private family discussion.

Dad: "Is that the best you can do?"

Eric: "Yes."

Jack: "And all you need is our signature, right?"

Eric: "I need your tax, title and license fees."

Jill: "How much is that?"

Eric: "The total is $1,060," he replied, turning over his proposal sheet, revealing the new information scribed by his manager in green Sharpie. "The financing is still subject to bank approval."

Dad: "I'm going to take care of the taxes for you two. Don't worry about that."

Jill: "Really? As it is, we can't go over $390, so I was hoping if we took the 84 month financing, the extra $5 would pay for the taxes."

Eric: "No, that would put you over $400 per month. In fact, we may have some issues already, since you have chosen not to put any money down. So you should at least take your dad up on his gener-ous offer," he counseled, hoping finally to get on Dad's good side.

Jill's dad knew he would do almost anything for his daughter and son-in-law. He just prayed he wouldn't have to cosign. He prayed even harder; Eric would refrain from bringing up the subject.

With the agreement now reached, Eric pulled out a credit appli-cation for Jack and Jill to fill out as he prepared the purchase and sale agreement. The form contained fields for all past residences as well as personal and financial references. When it came to the household income section, Jack had questions.

Jack: "I get a check, but it really only covers my health insurance and thirty-five hours a week at minimum wage. The rest is under the table."

Eric: "Just fill in the amount you can prove. The business manager will go over all that with you."

Eric had seen his business manager overcome all kinds of obstacles in securing lender approval. One technique involved submitting the finance application with all the household income included—provable or not. Once he had the loan approved, he would request the loan officer grant a proof of income waiver. Meaning, the bank would not call Jack's employer to verify the income on the application. This strategy proved less viable lately, however.

In any event, Eric wasn't about to get a bad attitude about the deal. At least he wouldn't show the Hills or his managers evidence of the rock that just dropped in his belly. Maybe Jill could go first on the loan application, with Jack as co-buyer. Maybe Dad would cosign. Just keep moving Eric, he thought to himself. I can't afford another mine deal this month. Mine deals occur when the bank steps on them and they blow up.

The Hills are looking at a $385 monthly payment on their new Crossover. As long as they have paid faithfully on the Mustang and the payment difference between the Mustang and Crossover are similar, banks are generally happy. This is but one piece of the loan's jigsaw puzzle or "structure," with which the dealership must contend. Dealerships practice structuring loan applications every day across America in order to secure approvals, deliver cars and make money.

Car Dealers *Structure* Loan Applications to Get You Approved

Structuring applications requires the dealership to reconcile the following:

1. The Hill's provable income.

2. Their mortgage obligations.

3. Their outstanding revolving credit card balances.

4. The amount of unused revolving credit still available to them.

However, the Hill's first and most prevalent problem is the size of the loan necessary to finance the Crossover, along with the four thousand dollars of negative equity still due on the Mustang. Many lenders will only advance between 100% and 110% of any vehicle's invoice, depending on the customer's credit. A vehicle that invoices for $20,000, such as the Crossover, can only receive a maximum advance of $22,000 from the lender. If all it took were $22,000 worth of loan advance to deliver the car, Eric would have an easy deal. But there are very few easy deals in today's market. Most times, applying for too large a vehicle loan (referred to as an "over-advance" in industry jargon) is enough to blow up a deal.

This takes us back to square one and the reasons salespeople ask those lousy questions you hate so much. Eric, his business manager and ABC motors must deal with a late inning game changer, which may anger the Hills sufficiently enough to drive them to the competition.

Here is how the Hills Crossover deal finance structure lays out on paper:

TABLE 13:   **How Negative Equity Causes Lender "Over Advance"**

	$23,435	Crossover M.S.R.P.
-	$1,500	Manufacturer's Rebate
-	$2,000	ABC Motors Advertised Discount
=	$19,935	Net Advertised Price
+	$4,000	Mustang Negative Equity
-	$0	Cash Down
=	$23,935	Loan Amount Needed
-	$22,035	Maximum Loan Advance
=	$1,900	Over Bank Lending Guidelines

Strike One: Attempting to borrow more than the maximum advance allowed by the bank's guidelines.

The next issue stems from the couple's expense structure at home. Again, Eric's manager wasn't there when the couple laid out their household finance plans, or when Jack agreed to under-the-table compensation. Nonetheless, it is the dealership's job to structure the information for a bank's approval. It takes three parties to agree: the dealer, the customer, and the bank. Only the dealer and customer are at the table, however. The bank is sitting behind a computer seemingly a million miles away. 75% to 80% of all customers rely on Eric and his bosses to figure all this stuff out and secure the loan. Otherwise folks such as the Hills become a statistic. Four out of five customers leave the dealership without ever taking delivery of a vehicle.

Here is how the Hills stack up at home:

TABLE 14:   **How Household Debt vs. Provable Household Income Affects Auto Lending**

	$7,083	True Household Monthly Income
−	$2,500	Jack's Under the Table Income
=	$4,583	Gross Taxable/Provable Monthly Income
−	$2,350	Monthly Home Mortgage
−	$350	Monthly Credit Card Payments
=	$1,883	Adjusted Household Income (AHI)
	$385	Proposed Crossover Payment
−	$320	17% of AHI or Maximum Car Payment
=	**$65**	**Per Month Over Bank Lending Guidelines**

Strike Two: Applying for a greater monthly payment than your provable household income and debt obligations will allow.

Strike Three: Asking a lender to stretch their guidelines on both of these issues simultaneously—especially when there is no down payment. No financial investment in the transaction other than a customer signature.

The Switch: Jerked Around *After* Negotiating for Three Hours

After the Hills signed the purchase and sale agreement and credit application, they sat at Eric's desk for fifteen minutes or so, before moving into the business manager's office. Following an introduction, the well-dressed manager rose from his office desk and extended his hand with a warm smile.

"My name is Luke. As Eric has probably told you, I am here to complete all your paperwork and secure your financing. Can I get you a cup of coffee?"

Jack, Jill and her father sat in the same type of semi-comfortable padded chairs to which they had been glued for most of the last two hours plus. No one said anything, but they were all a little tired of the excess sitting. And their eyeballs were floating from all the coffees and colas. They just wanted to sign what was necessary and get back to *Jeopardy* reruns.

"Unfortunately we heard back from three of our lenders electronically and there are two issues. First, you don't have enough provable income. Second, you are attempting to borrow $2,000 too much on the Crossover due to your Mustang's payoff."

Jill's dad jumped in; "Why don't you call them. Sometimes computers don't have the whole story," he appealed.

Luke: "I did, sir. Unfortunately that's what took me so long. I am sorry you had to wait for the results, but each of the three lenders said the same thing. Get a co-signer or find another vehicle that works."

Damn, her dad thought. *Maybe coming down to help the kids wasn't such a good idea.* A moment of silence ensued which Luke had been trained to honor.

"Well, somebody better make us a damned good deal on a Crossover the bank will finance, or we're heading straight over to XYZ Motors. My buddy at work has a brother that's a salesman over there," Jill's dad threatened. Jill knew he was upset. The veins sticking out of his neck were a telling sign.

Luke: "Eric, would you show the Hills one of those two lovely Program Crossovers we have out there? I should have a conditional approval by the time they have test-driven it."

This was not Luke's first day at the rodeo. He switched vehicles on customers dozens of times per month. The only time he missed was when salespeople such as Eric failed to offer switch cars earlier on in the process. In this case Eric had offered the program rental car as a means to save the couple $5,000. He did so, before even presenting the new Crossover numbers. The Hills had declined at the time. However, because Eric had at least mentioned the idea earlier, the suggestion didn't appear so ominous. It didn't feel like a last-ditch effort to cram them into something they didn't want. It didn't hurt their ego.

In this case, Jill's dad became the dealership's biggest advocate. Luke did say he would either need a cosigner *or* get an approval on one of these program cars. So the couple took the 12,000 mile, current model year, fleet game buy-back Crossover for a test drive. Jill's dad provided assurance that the program car might be a better deal. He was right in some respects. The payment would be lower.

However, the couple's upside-down situation would grow immediately from $4,000 on the Mustang—to $8,000 on the Crossover—the exact moment they signed the papers.

But the couple got a Crossover. They even lowered their payments down from $385 on the Mustang to $350 on the program car. Still not the $269 they saw in the ad, and not the $300 they had budgeted. Nevertheless, it was less than the $385 the new one would have cost them. This was no small feat, after increasing their interest rate from the Mustang's 1.9% APR financing, to the Crossover's 6.9% rate. All the more interest they'll owe the bank. All the more they will owe when they trade it back in three years from now—less than half-way through their loan. Rocks are hard, water is wet, and the Hills will never see the title to that car. They will trade it before they pay it off.

Ironically, the nemesis of rental cars—which killed their Mustang's resale value and kept the couple from getting a loan on a new Crossover—proved to be their temporary salvation. It is this circular relationship that simultaneously keeps the industry in bond-age yet on sufficient life-support to sell cars. It perpetuates its own peril by selling you a vehicle—one that makes it nearly impossible to sell you another—*for a long, long, time.*

In the Hills' case, like in countless others, the automaker bailed out of another fleet game car and the dealer made a $2,000 profit sell-ing a used vehicle, instead of breaking even on a new ad car. As a result, the union got to stay on the production line, rather than sit home and watch *Oprah.* The Hills are among the 80% who end up purchas-ing something other than what they came in to buy and among the 80% who trade in a car while doing so. They are among the 80% who require financing through the dealership and among 100% of those driving their negative equity problem higher and higher each time they buy. Amazing.

The program Crossover came with the remaining factory war-ranty, entitling the Hills to another four years and 48,000 miles of original coverage. They, like all customers, will need it. They will also need ABC Motors to remain vibrant and profitable, or those inevitable service experiences could prove miserable. Car companies don't make it easy for dealerships like ABC to make money. They really draw no connection between ABC's financial success and its ability to care for customers like Jack and Jill Hill. In the end, however, like it or not, automakers are the boss.

Ten

How the Automobile Franchise System Works

... and Why the Dealer is Not Always the Boss

*"You can find your way across this
country using burger joints the
way a navigator uses stars."*

—CHARLES KURALT
Award-winning Journalist (1934–1997)

T he closest analogy to the way the automobile franchise system works is the fast food business. Let's take McDonald's, Wendy's and Burger King for example; all individual companies competing in the fast food burger business. Each represents their own "brand" of restaurant. They advertise their brands to the consumer by differentiating; cooking methods, flavor, convenience, price, and even premium movie collectibles available only at their locations.

While some of these restaurants are owned by the companies themselves, most of their stores are independently owned and operated. This means regular people like you and me—if so inclined and cash endowed—are able to make contracts with them, in order to sell their particular kind of burgers, fries, and shakes. These written understandings are known as franchise agreements. The company, such as

Burger King, is the "franchisor," and the individual owner/operator is the "franchisee." For our purposes, let's use Burger King and a mythical franchisee named Patty Cake.

Burger King's franchise agreements include a company-approved location, facility architecture, and an interior design plan for construction of the restaurant. From approved mechanical equipment to the employee uniforms, operations are tightly specified in order to offer the brand experience Burger King wishes to project. The agreement stipulates which goods and other supplies must be purchased directly from Burger King by Patty, as well as Patty's compensation to Burger King for all the advertising and brand imaging it has developed.

Some compensation models might require Patty to purchase a minimum amount of beef, rolls, potatoes, etc., in any given period. Alternately, they may call for a forwarding of a set percentage of the store's sales dollars back to Burger King. The contracts also carve out a defined territory for Patty as the franchisee. This protects her from additional Burger King restaurants being placed within her market.

In addition to perfecting every paragraph of her franchise contract, Patty is responsible for all the financial risks and commitments associated with construction and operation of "her" restaurant. She is responsible for securing all the facility construction financing, inventory financing, and her working capital requirements. This entails either a tremendous investment of personal wealth by Patty or a sizable risk by the bank that finances her; often both. Should Patty's business fail, Burger King has no further obligation to Patty, aside from perhaps the repurchase of some unspoiled inventory and signage.

When a franchised burger joint or dealership goes under, the entrepreneur suffers, not the franchisor. Interestingly enough—now edified by the failures of GM and Chrysler—if Burger King itself were ever to fail for reasons outside of Patty's control, she still suffers.

If Patty Cake wishes to sell or transfer her business to another person or entity for whatever reason, Burger King has a right to either accept or reject the deal. When the purpose of the sale is to avoid imminent business failure, waiting for the approval of the company can be lethal. Many times, franchise owners expend significant time and resources negotiating a sale with someone who will never be approved by the company. Some companies use this tool to help manage their franchisee network.

This happens especially when franchisors, like those in the car industry, include the "right of first refusal" in their agreements. This drastically reduces the number of potential buyers for the business. Few buyers are willing to go through the costly exercise of negotiating a complicated deal, only to have the company steal it away. Often franchisor motivations for such clauses emanate from a desire for authority to permanently close the location or award it to a favored candidate. Harley-Davidson, for example, keeps a list of preapproved dealer candidates. Dealers wishing to sell their locations are wise to consult Harley first. Otherwise, a long, drawn-out deal approval process often results in a dead-end.

This really harms business owners and their deserved exit strategies. Less potential suitors to purchase an individual's business, means less buyer price competition for the business. This, of course, results in the franchisee receiving far less for his or her business than would otherwise be gained, if the company left this clause out of the franchise agreement.

Very little of a franchise agreement is negotiable by the franchisee, however. Most of the contract content is weighted against the franchisee and is self-serving to the parent company. Language artfully provides all kinds of "kick-out" and franchise cancellation provisions for the franchisor and very little protection for the independent businessperson. This is frustrating to the Patty Cakes of the world, given they must put most or all of their family's finances at risk, in order to gain approval for the franchise. Investments become a scary endeavor for both investors and their banks if the company retains the option of terminating the relationship at will. One can only imagine the personal financial devastation that would occur if franchisors could terminate and relocate local businesses on a whim. In the car business, the federal government has figured out a way to do just that; blowing past secured creditor contracts and franchise contracts in order to achieve its agenda.

Of course, if too many of a company's franchised locations fail, the pool of likely replacements and their bankers dry up quickly. There are too many other places to invest capital, time, and effort, other than in a franchise with a risky reputation. This aside, once the franchise system sets its legs, the franchisor (the company) is off the hook. The franchisee—on the other hand—is all in, often with no place to go if things don't work out. Personally guaranteed credit instruments are often a prerequisite of the bank's loan approval. This means owner/operator homes are also on the table and up for grabs in case of business failure. The cause of such failure is unimportant to lenders. It could be for any reason including franchisor failure, franchisee failure, or government-forced business closings such as with GM and Chrysler.

Who Wants a Franchise? Get 'Em While Their Hot!

So why would anyone want to get into bed with these franchise characters? Simple. The franchise system supports anyone wishing to build a burger joint, a car dealership, or the like, with instant brand identity. If Ragsdale Burgers advertised a two-for-one burger deal, sales would probably go up. But if McDonald's promotes this kind of deal, look out!

Franchises make the businessperson more identifiable and recognizable. Franchises provide instant validity, credibility, and exposure to any business. Banks can more easily benchmark the expected financial performance of a franchised business, making them more likely to approve business loans. Independent joints like Ragsdale Burgers or used car lots are riskier bets.

The franchisor company, either burger or automaker, trademarks specific products. Diners cannot buy a Whopper at McDonald's or

Wendy's. In this same spirit, automobile consumers can only buy new Fords, like the Mustang, at a franchised Ford dealership.

Similar to fast food chains, the automobile franchise system ensures consumers maintain not only choices between Wendy's, McDonald's, and Burger King, but also choices between different car locations offering the same exact products. If a customer doesn't like the deal or warranty service she receives at her hometown Chevrolet dealer, she can travel a town or two away and find another Chevrolet dealer. This, of course, assumes there is another Chevrolet dealer managing to stay in business, despite all the challenges. Such freedom of choice in auto retail is becoming a thing of the past, however. If the market or the automakers aren't closing dealerships, the government is.

I don't pretend to understand the ins and outs of a franchised burger restaurant. I haven't worked in or operated one for 25 seconds, never mind 25 years. Nor have I calculated the impact they have on our freedom of choice or a taxpayer's household economy. However, I do know a thing or two about car dealers and the vast array of purchasing choices they provide the American public.

The only way to get a brand new car or truck in the U.S.A. is through a franchised car or truck dealer. Automobile manufacturers build cars and then "wholesale" them to the dealers to whom they have awarded a franchise. Due to one of the few *effective* small business protection laws, auto manufacturers and distributors cannot and do not sell to anyone but their dealers. No matter whether you are a huge corporation, registering thousands of vehicles per year, or someone driving their vehicle for ten years before trading it in; all consumers have an equal choice between some 20,000 dealerships in this country. Sadly, we have lost some 4,000 dealership locations in the last twenty years. Even more alarming is the loss of some 1,000 dealers in 2008 alone!

The industry originally projected the loss of some 2,000 additional dealers in 2009, primarily due to market conditions. With 340 failing in the first three months of 2009 and 789 Chrysler, Dodge, and Jeep dealers receiving termination letters, that number will be easily eclipsed. 1,124 General Motors dealers also received such love letters from their automaker the announcing the non-renewal of their franchise contracts in October 2010. These terminations were irrespective of dealership mortgages outstanding or the personal loan guarantees signed by owner/operators.

Nonetheless, this takes the total dealership population down to 18,000 locations, an insufficient number to service and replace some 250 million cars on American roads today. In any event, the more that fail, or are forced out of business by government-run automakers, the fewer choices American consumers retain. Fewer choices *always* mean higher prices, if Mr. Reidy's doughnut auctions taught me anything.

While our franchise system is not perfect and gives consumers great grief at times, it is truly the only way to ensure we all protect our freedom of choice in a free market society. Forgive the drama, but if any one entity controls both manufacturing and retail pricing, consumers would pay the monopolized highest price. They would have but one place to service and that would be the monopolized standard. The way things look now, the federal government will be that controlling entity. Freedom meets Socialism and her little brother Tyranny. I doubt any of us will get along the same.

Some of you may retort, "Yes, but at least I would know I was paying the same as everyone else and not getting screwed." To you I reply: if you take a moment to grasp what is really going on in this industry, you would realize the car dealer is the least of your worries. If you enjoy the service line at Wal-Mart to resolve an issue with your TV or toaster oven, you will love the manner in which a factory or government-owned store deals with your automotive issues.

What Happened to the Small Dealer with Great Service?

Your local car dealer/franchisee is one of the following:

1. A second or third generation operator—son or daughter.
2. A minority gaining or having gained ownership through a factory sponsored buyout program.

3. A former dealership manager who found a financial backer or some other financing.

4. A large public corporation having amassed a chain of stores.

5. An outsider who brought a lot of money into his new dealership endeavor.

6. A factory insider who received favor on a right-of-first-refusal deal, often accompanied by insider captive financing-arm considerations.

When car dealers are unable to stay in business, the greatest loss to you, the consumer, is the loss of the little guy. He or she typically provides the best service and community focus in the industry. They keep the big guys honest because the small dealer has a better handle on the pulse of what his employees practice. However, he cannot survive like the "Megadealers" can. These are multi-franchise, multi-location operators who maintain the ability to fund their poorly performing dealerships from the coffers of more profitable stores. Megadealers often own dealerships representing some highly profitable brands. They also represent franchises that lose money every month of every year. Nevertheless, at the end of each period, they stay liquid enough with the profitable franchises in order to hang onto the dogs.

Still, a big guy like Bill Heard, Jr., who owned and operated a fourteen-store chain of Chevrolet dealerships in the southern states, filed Chapter 11 bankruptcy in 2008. Company spokespeople claim the financial failure was due to a national loss of the truck market and an inability to place sub-prime (risky credit) loans with lenders. Heard did not have a Lexus, BMW, or several Honda and Toyota franchises—as do many megadealers—to offset his bleeding Chevrolet dealerships.

Minneapolis megadealer Denny Hecker has recently closed his stores and has been sued personally by both Chrysler Credit and Hyundai Financial. Chrysler has succeeded in receiving a multimillion dollar judgment. This means virtually anything Hecker has built or taken home throughout his career will surely be lost.

All this makes the dealership a risky investment. Risky investments don't often invite well-heeled investors, talented business operators, or their banks to the party. At periods of market highs, dealers with popular brands make a lot of money. At periods of market lows, they often give it all back and more. The right manufacturer for a dealer to represent is more an issue of *when* than *which*. Timing is everything. Today's hot sellers can and do easily fall cold. For example: just prior to my family's first foray into the Pontiac business in 1992, Pontiac touted itself as the third-highest volume car company (cars only, no trucks) in the marketplace, just behind BMW. Today, the entire brand is being shuttered. No global player even wants to buy it.

How Much Money Do Car Dealers Make?

If the economy is important to American taxpayers and workers, it is vital they have some basic understanding of how the auto industry uses its dealers to collectively move $675 billion in annual sales of goods and services. Dealers employ over 1.1 million workers as salespeople, managers, technicians, and parts and office personnel.[15] The annual employee payroll for all franchised dealers approximates $53 billion directly into the U.S. economy.[16]

These clear and honorable financial contributions do not come easily. Dealer net profit margins average just 1.5% on sales. This means for every $100 in goods and services a dealer sells, he takes just a $1.50 to his bottom line net profit. Viewed another way, if a car dealer gives away $100 worth of mud flaps to a customer, he must sell $6,750 in additional goods and services to pay for it. In some cases that's an entire used car or 100 hours of technician labor sales to pay for a cruddy pair of mud flaps. Perhaps that can put things in a perspective you can accept and understand.

In the last few years the average dealer sold $31 to $33 million in goods and services annually.[17] That sounds like a lot and it is. He retained roughly one-tenth of that money after paying for his inventory (new cars, used cars, parts, and technicians labor time), which is still a lot of money; around $4 million annually. However, he still hasn't paid for any of his operating expenses.

$32 million in sales - $26 million cost of goods sold = $4 million *gross* profit (before expenses).

The $4 million represents the amount an average car dealer has left over to operate his dealership. Running dealerships is an expensive endeavor however. On average, it costs some $3.5 million annually. Some major expenses:

Employee payroll:	$2.5 million
Dealer advertising:	$365,000
Rent or mortgage interest:	$335,000
Inventory interest (floorplan) charges:	$200,000

All of this activity culminates in an average bottom-line net profit of around $40,000 per month. This may sound like a lot of money to many business owners and it is. Likewise, consumers hold little sympathy for businesses making this large a profit. Perhaps we can agree, however, that a half-million dollars per year is far less than anyone assumes car dealers make. In fairness, some large metropolitan dealers, operating with hot products in affluent consumer markets can make ten times this amount. But the average is the average. Meaning, for every one anomaly earning this kind of money, there are several hundred dealerships making far less than a half-million per year.

If the industry, his local market or his brand recedes by thirty percent, the dealer's gross profit is reduced by $1.2 million dollars and the dealership begins losing money. The numbers hold true mathematically

in cases of dealerships with annual sales volumes from \$20 million to
\$100 million. If not remedied quickly, the dealership fails: one less
place for consumers to shop.

Typically, however, recessions cut dealer new vehicle sales in half.
At this level, unless the dealer can increase used vehicle sales or service
sales to compensate, dealership operations hemorrhage violently. At
these times, lenders get nervous and either increase floorplan interest rates or terminate the dealer's credit relationship altogether. The
smallest dealers fail first, as they typically have less leverage against the
bank and often have no other outside sources of cash flow to keep the
business solvent.

Robert Nardelli, former CEO of the Home Depot and now
former Chrysler LLC chief (prebankruptcy), reported to Congress
that 250 Chrysler dealers were on credit-hold through the second
quarter of 2008. This meant those dealers were unable to purchase
any more vehicles from Chrysler because their banks shut off their
inventory loans. These dealers employed 13,250 workers, and they
could not buy inventory to resell. How did they pay their employees?
They simply ran out of cash and failed.

How did this affect Chrysler? First, few if any investors or their
banks want to purchase and finance one of their franchised dealerships. Therefore, they are in business with the dealers they had in
the game, relying upon them to buy all the cars Chrysler would ever
build. Second, those existing dealers—upon whom Chrysler relied to
take those cars—were failing. A failing dealership cannot take more
cars from their manufacturer. So Chrysler could not stay in business
either.

Why You and the Industry Need as Many Dealerships as Possible

Ironically and nonsensically, the 789 dealers just terminated by
Chrysler—via the federal government's task force recommendations—
ranged well beyond the 250 on credit-hold. Many of the terminated

dealers managed to continue making money or breaking even during these tough times. Now, instead of having just 250 less dealers to buy and sell manufactured cars, the Wall Street whiz kids decided it was better to amp that number up closer to 800. Tragically flawed thinking I'm afraid.

How does this affect you the consumer? Other than perhaps altruistic concern for all the folks who build, sell, and fix Chryslers; very little. Customers will go the way of those once driving Packards, Plymouths, and Oldsmobiles. They will just buy something else. But we are not just talking about one brand. We are talking about an entire industry. Toyota was down by over 30% in the fourth quarter of 2008 and posted $7.7 billion in losses from January through March of 2009. This was their first loss in over 70 years. Do you see Toyota sending out termination letters to dealers? No. Why? Because Toyota realizes it needs its dealers to be successful. Toyota knows there is no correlation between *its* current financial losses and accountability to its dealer network. Toyota knows what it is doing.

Alternatively, the Wall Street whiz kids wielding the power of the federal government clearly do not. They feel by modeling the Toyota game-plan and imposing it upon the domestics, better things will happen. They are wrong. After they close these dealerships, the damage will be done, and it will be too late.

Dealers do not close their operations and simply reopen at a later date due to clearer thinking or court intervention. The legal, financial, employment, and licensing requirements are far too complicated for that. But even for those dealerships that remain, satisfying customers is no easy feat. It's not that consumers are unreasonably difficult to satisfy. It is really a matter of automakers getting out of their dealers' way—encouraging them to do the right things for customers—instead of punishing them as a means to save money.

Eleven

How Automakers Prevent Dealers from Keeping You Happy

... and Think They're Saving Money by Doing So

> *"Regard your soldiers as your children and they will follow you into the deepest valleys. Look on them as your own beloved sons, and they will stand by you even unto death!"*
> —SUN TZU, *The Art of War*
> Military Tactician & Author (544 B.C.–481 B.C.)

The single biggest factor influencing a car dealer's success is the manufacturer he represents. The right brand can make a mediocre dealer a millionaire. The wrong one can and does bankrupt even the greatest of operators. The idea of right and wrong automaker, as you now know, is really a matter of timing. Own the right franchise, at the right time, and life gets easier. However, whether the industry or a given brand is boom or bust, manufacturer's attitudes toward their dealers are generally lousy.

This of course, creates terrible repercussions for the consumer. Why? Manure rolls downhill. An unhappy boss makes unhappy workers, who put out a lousy product or service. Lousy products or services disenfranchise customers. A disenfranchised customer is a lost customer. Period.

The problem is really one of perspective. Automakers' management jobs may be on the line (or at least they should be), but their dealers' entire financial future is on the line. They have pledged their home, along with the rest of their personal assets, in order to get a loan and represent their manufacturer. I am sure you know the difference between a chicken and a pig when it comes to your breakfast? The chicken is "involved" with your breakfast. The pig is "committed." The federal government may bail out banks and automakers. But dealers are off the radar screen, unless of course, they are targeted for a termination letter as part of somebody's boardroom plan.

This is not an equitable business relationship and, thus, not a partnership at all. And when car companies send in condescending contact managers to strong-arm their dealers into the latest management fad, the "partnership" reference becomes a joke. If automakers could ever be a fly on the wall and hear how dealers speak of them at dealer-only meetings, they would be horrified. How can this be a good working relationship? It can't. It isn't. And the customer suffers the most—particularly in the service lane.

Automakers' dealer policy and procedure manuals lay a common cord of well thought-out processes outlining how dealers get paid. Dealers must follow these steps in order to both receive and keep factory-to-dealer reimbursements for items such as warranty repairs and customer rebates. While necessary to have in some form or fashion, the books functionally serve as a quagmire of "gotchas" that offer no benefit whatsoever to the dealer or the retail customer. They do however, leave the door wide open for the factory to audit and recover a good chunk of otherwise rightful dealer reimbursement money back. This occurs virtually whenever they want, or need, the money, and negatively affects the way you are treated when your vehicle needs a warranty repair from a dealership.

Dealers front the factory for both the rebates they offer customers and the warranty repairs dealers perform on customer's vehicles. Customers receive their manufacturer's rebates at the point of sale, leaving dealers to bill the factory for reimbursement later on. Likewise, dealers purchase warranty repair parts from the manufacturer up front and pay their technicians to install them—then bill the factory for the work later.

How Automakers Offer Massive Rebates
& Fix Your Warranty Problems for Free!

The story doesn't end once the manufacturers get around to paying the dealers their due reimbursements. In most states, the automakers have the relatively unfettered ability to audit, review and retract these payments for up to one year following dealer payment. Therefore, factory audits are punitive at the least and at worst, cause dealer financial failure. Most audits are controlled by the automaker's national office. However, they can be requested, diverted or thrown in the waste basket by factory managers playing political games at their discretion. My first taste of an audit occurred some twenty years ago.

In 1989, my dad's Chevrolet dealership was audited for the purpose of reviewing rebates paid during the summer of 1988. With very little notice, GM's audit team arrived at the store, demanding production of all our "deal jackets" for the period under examination. (deal jacket refers to the file folders that contain all the paperwork pertaining to customer purchase transactions)

My father couldn't possibly anticipate the way Chevrolet and General Motors were intending to cheat him, by charging back a great number of rebates he had fronted customers at GM's behest. Some of the "gotcha" triggers are simple: Is the proper rebate amount reflected on the signed and executed customer purchase and sale agreement? Did the customer sign the rebate form to grant the dealer proper authorization to collect the rebate? These are basic steps to protect dealer income and I have a tough time feeling badly for any dealer who gets nicked over simple stuff.

In my father's case, however, GM's audit team took a look at the date of the customer's GMAC finance application and approvals, as well as the date of the internal predelivery inspection repair order and state inspection sticker. They even looked at the date of the gas purchase order used for a complimentary initial fill-up of the customer's new vehicle at the pump. These documents were important to the auditors in order to make the case that we gave customers rebates *after* the rebate period ended. The auditors left my father an $18,000 bill.

The automakers' practice of running rebate programs through the weekends makes sense. At that time, even more so than today, Saturdays and Sundays were prime customer shopping days. Too bad GMAC did not staff its desks with loan officers having authority to approve auto loans on weekends. Too bad their supervisors didn't work Saturdays like dealers must, due to their "executive" status. And too bad for my dad, because by the time GMAC got around to making a positive loan decision on Monday, the rebate period had ended.

However, the customers had agreed to the figures offered when the rebate period was in force. The idea of asking the customer to pay more because GMAC went golfing on the weekends was preposterous. GM offered the deal, GMAC messed around with the loan application, and GM still got the deal. Since GM owned GMAC at the time (the folks responsible for the delay), the inability of the dealer to deliver the car during the rebate period was GM's fault. Are you getting the math? The guys who approved and enjoyed the fruits of the sale and the profits of the loan's interest income, later extricated themselves from the financial obligations of reimbursing their dealer.

My father went ballistic. "They get you to sell your vehicles below cost this way," he said. "If I sold the car for a $1,000 profit and they take their $1,500 rebate away, then I lost $500 to sell a car for them! If the customer bought the car on Saturday and picked it up on Monday after his financing was approved, why should I lose money? They can't go get it back from the customer, so they nail us for it!" He was right.

I was not so fortunate in a General Motors warranty audit, however. Just one month after I closed on the purchase of my dad's Chevrolet store, the audit squad showed up to bless me with a $65,000 bill. When the lead auditor came in and introduced himself, he said they were there to "help me with some of our warranty procedures." I knew the kind of help he meant.

Similar to Dad's sales audit when we pulled out all the deal jackets, we dragged out thousands of warranty repair-order documents for auditor review. In my particular case, half of the issues the auditors noted stemmed from flushing transmissions without using the GM-approved flushing device. The technicians had figured out how to save time doing it a different way. None of the transmissions had ever come back for repeat repairs, mind you. This fact was irrelevant to the auditors, however. A bulletin had been sent out by the factory— one of dozens they send out weekly—and we didn't follow the exact procedure, so "tough cookies."

We had also replaced some brake rotors due to customer complaints about their car shaking under braking. And rather than have our customers drive their vehicles in a state of disrepair, we had given them loaner cars over the weekend. The factory was up in arms about this practice, because they did not categorize the issue as a safety item, proving once again they are far too often penny-wise and pound-foolish. $70 in rental fees, apparently, is far too much to pay for a customer feeling safe and feeling satisfied.

The factory was equally disturbed by what they termed as "repeat repair attempts." Technicians attempt to make a correct diagnosis by identifying failed components, then replacing them with new parts. If the new part does not correct the situation, logic would say the dealer should try something else—like finding another culprit. However, if he does replace a second part, the factory categorizes the claim as a "multiple parts replacement attempt." This means if the second effort actually fixed the customer's particular issue, they don't like to reimburse the dealer for the parts and labor used on the first attempt.

GM was already paid for the parts that were now on our customer's vehicles. The technicians were already paid for the work. Some of the transactions were a year old, ten or eleven months prior to my even purchasing and owning the company. Again, "tough cookies."

The most frustrating and arbitrary policy GM and other manufacturers maintain in their warranty policy is the need for "The Three
C's," which stand for "Cause, Cure and Correction." This requirement
turns dealership technicians into reincarnations of John Steinbeck.
This means they must write an elaborate story not only to justify
everything they do in fixing a customer's complaint, but why they did
it. Automotive technicians are not at the dealership to author another
The Grapes of Wrath. They are there to fix cars and, by default, satisfy customers. However, according to GM and most manufacturers,
if their story is not documented in an acceptable manner—and to an
auditor's satisfaction—the claim is charged back.

Additionally, the auditors grabbed us for not having technicians
perform a cost-saving analysis of the feasibility in repairing the failed
part, rather than replacing it. Forget the Steinbeck novel, let's require
our techs to publish a thesis. That ought to keep them focused on
what's important—factory nonsense—instead of the customer's
interests. The auditors said their goodbyes after three terrifying days
of microinspection. I've had gentler colonoscopies.

Later that month I was served notice that my Pontiac-Cadillac
store was also going to be audited due to "common ownership." Ironic,
given I didn't own the Chevrolet dealership during the period being
audited. Nonetheless, the audit team tagged me with another $35,000
in charge-backs, due to nearly identical procedural errors on the
Pontiac-Cadillac dealership's part. I did have a small victory in getting a
few of the charge backs thrown out, thanks to state statutes which limit
factories to a one-year look-back from the claim submission date. This
protection sticks as long as the factory cannot prove dealer fraud.

Some dealers cheat and steal from the factory. I was never one
of them. Regardless, in October 2002, GM removed over $90,000
from my dealerships' bank accounts via their mandatory electronic
access privileges granted in their franchise agreement. When the factory comes like a thief in the night for her money, she need neither
knock on the dealership's door nor pick the lock. There are no factory
receivables administrators calling my dealership payables controller.

Nobody needed me to sign a check. Instead, the automakers maintain open, unilateral access to their dealer's checking accounts. They make reimbursement payments and withdrawals according to their own clock. The manufacturers giveth and the manufacturers taketh away. Gangstah Pleeeease!

How Their Plan Hurts Both You and Them

Most importantly to folks like the Hills of the world, GM suspended our warranty self-authorization privileges. This required us to tie up customers' vehicles longer, as we waited for factory approval to repair their cars. Nothing aggravates customers faster than service dissatisfaction. "Customers reporting a positive service experience are eight times as likely to purchase their next vehicle from the same dealer," according to Garry Palmer, President of ODS Consulting, in Palm City, Florida. Operating in an "I can't fix your car today" mode leaves customers stranded. They end up leaving the dealership and abandoning the brand itself. Automakers miss this point. Repair restrictions and audits are great ways for factories to grab a quick and substantial cash infusion, all at dealer and retail customer expense. They look no further than the immediate gratification of an $80,000 per year auditor recovering some $20,000 per day from their dealers. In truth, they cannot buy the audit money back in either dealer or consumer blood. Manure still rolls downhill.

This is all about priorities. For the entire cavity search GM performed on my Pontiac-Cadillac dealership's warranty documents, they recovered just $35,000. The charge-back amounted to roughly 5% of our annual factory warranty labor and parts revenue. GM being overcharged 5%, in order to ensure their customers are satisfied, was apparently viewed as a budgetary abomination. This amount could be arguably lost on three or four Pontiac Grand Ams beginning their life in the fleet game. Depreciating customers' cars through rebate and fleet games—Check. Stealing dealer income to subsidize known component problems and rebate offerings—Check. Jerking customers around in the service lane—Check. Encouraging customers to defect to other brands—Checkmate!

The auditors "helped" us by removing a big chunk of dealership working capital, along with discouraging my employees from satisfying our customers. In this sadly contentious relationship between automakers and their dealers, the problems with warranty work are both bizarre and exhausting. And the ultimate loser of the battle is the customer.

Jack and Jill's First Service Visit

It had been about two months since Jack said goodbye to his Mustang and began driving Jill's Civic to work each day. It felt like trading Armani loafers for a pair of used Payless sandals, but he took solace in the extra protection Jill and their unborn baby would enjoy by commuting in the Crossover. That was until Jill began complaining about a pulsation in her brakes. Vibrations ran up her arms through the steering wheel on every stop. She felt unsafe. Jack took the car for a spin and concurred. After all, the whole point of enduring the negotiation nightmare was the safety of his family. He wanted the car fixed, with no stories.

Eric had introduced the Hills to a service advisor at the time of their Crossover delivery. Jack had called her for an appointment, but was told by the young lady to "just bring it in." So he did, entering through the showroom though, in order to grab Eric for support. After reviewing the complaint, Jack's service advisor extracted the service manager from his back office so he, Jack and Eric could take a diagnostic ride together in the Crossover.

"I can feel it too," the manager said. "We have seen this before. The metallic brake pad manufacturers use softer, less heat resistant material than the old asbestos pads used to be. So the rotors get hotter. When you hit a puddle while the rotors are hot, they have a tendency to warp."

"Does that mean it's not covered under warranty?" Jack inquired.

"It means our factory service representative will have to look at it *before* we make the repair. The decision is his to make. Either he pays, you pay, or the dealership pays—usually a combination of all three. But it's his call. I will give you a 1-800 customer service number to contact, which usually helps to get a ruling in your favor. I can't call the number for you. It is reserved for customers only," the manager answered.

"Will that help getting it fixed today"? Jack replied.

"Possibly. They will still want the factory guy to look at it; and being a Friday, it is unlikely the rep can make it in here before the weekend."

"Great." Jack retorted with a tinge of frustration. "Can I get a different car to use over the weekend? I don't want my pregnant wife driving it this way."

"We can put you into a rental car over the weekend. But that will be on your credit card. From the factory's point of view, the car is still drivable, even though it feels unsafe. I will get the general manager to help you out with some of that expense on the dealership's dime. But unless you argue a good case with the 1-800 people, the factory is unlikely to pay anything for the rental."

Jack picked up one of those ugly family vans (that Jill hated so much) for her to drive over the weekend, or until the factory and dealer could get their act together. He was formerly unaware, but becoming educated in the politics of warranty repair. ABC could have told Jack there was no problem, the loaner was free, and the vehicle would be repaired by tomorrow.

However, dealers like ABC have become more and more restricted in their ability to do the right thing. Automakers trip over dollars to pick up nickels, while losing customers through a very complicated warranty system; one designed like *The Matrix*. They monitor and graph the frequency of every possible classification and category of repair against similar-sized dealer "peer groups," as well as national warranty repair cost per vehicle averages. Finding a dealer anywhere

out of line in any area generates factory interest in further investiga-
tion and audits.

But folks like Jack and Jill Hill don't care about ratios and averages
or peer groups or factory contact managers' weekend plans. They just
want their car fixed.

Twelve

Why Dealership Service Departments are So Expensive

... Yet Surprisingly Fail to Make Big Profits

*"The company in which you improve
most will be the least expensive to you."*

—GEORGE WASHINGTON
First U.S. President (1732–1799)

utomobile technicians are a breed in and among themselves. They have the toughest job in the dealership, bar none. How a human being can stand on his or her feet all day, cantered into an upper back-bend, while being dripped on by the wet and grimy underbelly of an automobile is beyond me. Nevertheless, these folks just love fixing cars. They also, for the most part, love making money.

The larger issue with getting good technicians to join dealerships is their brand specificity. Vehicles differ greatly from brand to brand. The days of knowing how to work on an engine, transmission, or perform general maintenance have gone away. Many manufacturers will only pay a warranty claim, for example, if the dealership tech holds certification for the specific repair job being performed. This makes job-jumping technicians think twice about changing brands.

In order for a dealer to entice a technician to jump for more pay, he must first be certain the tech will produce sufficient labor hours and labor income for both himself and the dealership. It is difficult to keep an expensive tech's dance card full, when he lacks certifications to do a lot of the work. So dealers often give them pay "guarantees" for a period of time until they bone up on their needed courses.

Most techs work on a flat-rate system. This means they are assigned jobs carrying a predetermined time allowance to complete. The time allowances are all published in a book. The referenced time allowance dictates both what technicians are paid and what customers are charged, regardless of the actual time it takes a tech to complete the work. Some job times are more liberal than others. Techs learn which jobs pay well, but can be completed in very little time.

Techs learning the best paying jobs weigh, measure, and monitor the types of work the service manager or job dispatcher gives them in relation to the other techs in the shop. For example, customer pay work pays by the book. Warranty work also pays by the book. However, the customer books such as Chilton's or Mitchell's pay 25% more time for the same job than the manufacturer's warranty book. So it stands to reason, technicians prefer customer cash pay work over warranty work. Managers typically use cash work favors as a means to placate, appease, or punish technicians. Likewise, techs embroiled for most of a day or week on a tough warranty job may be ingratiated with some cash "gravy" work in order to make up for the torture and loss of income.

Dealers can count on the relative stability of income derived from the service and parts departments. New and Used vehicle sales are extremely volatile, rising and dipping more sharply. However, for the hourly rate that's charged, one would assume that dealers make a mint in their service shops. Not so fast.

The mass merchandisers such as Midas, Speedy, Jiffy, Sears, BJ's, and Wal-Mart don't perform difficult diagnostics and warranty work. Why? There is no profit in the technical stuff. It requires too much training, too much diagnostic equipment, and technicians commanding high wages. Consequently, they leave the tough stuff up to the dealers to lose money on. Dealers have difficulty charging an hourly rate low enough to sell the competitive work of mass merchandisers, but high enough to afford paying the expensive technicians necessary to complete troubling repairs. Mass merchandisers typically hire and train vocational mechanics who are capable of performing the maintenance type jobs these entities offer. Such workers are employable at a much lower rate than more highly-educated dealership technicians. Mass merchandisers need not worry about a slew of manufacturer special tool investments and certification requirements. Short of a governmental issue, they are not subject to audit. They sell generic parts purchased from negotiated suppliers.

Their entire overhead expense structure is incomparable to the franchised dealer. They can charge less and do so more profitably. Consequently, they have forced dealers to accommodate this price suppression by discounting dealership labor on the type of jobs dealers used to rely upon for profits. The best example is the $29.95 oil change. Assuming $15 in oil and filter costs, that leaves roughly $15 in labor charges. Take a look at the following table, which lays out the difference in profitability between mass merchandisers and dealerships charging the same $15 labor charge:

TABLE 15:   **Dealership vs. Mass Merchandiser Profit Margins**

	Dealership	Mass Merchandiser
Labor Charge	$15.00	$15.00
Tech Pay Per Hour	$20.00	$12.00
Time Paid Tech in Hours	0.33	0.33
Tech $ Pay	$6.60	$3.96
Gross Profit	$8.40	$11.04
Gross Profit Margin	**56%**	**74%**

At 20 minutes per job, a technician can perform three oil changes per hour. $15 labor charge per oil change x 3 oil changes per hour = $45 effective hourly shop rate. Many dealers do not calculate the math on items such as oil changes. They assume they are collecting the hourly rate posted by the service manager. This is not true. In fact, in order for the dealership to maintain the same gross profit margin as the mass merchandiser, he must either pay his technicians an identical amount or raise his hourly oil change rate to $75 per hour.

If you were investing in a company, would you rather put your money in one operating on a 56% gross profit margin while suffering large operating expense overhead and revenue audits, or perhaps into one operating at a 73% gross profit margin with lower expenses and little risk?

In fact, dealers would have to charge $40 for their oil changes to retain the same margins as mass merchandisers. This is not possible, because the oil change market is set between $26.95 and $29.95. I know we are talking small numbers here. But let's expand the differences out over a year in the average dealership shop:

TABLE 16:   **Shop Profitability Measured Over a Year's Time**

	Dealership	Mass Merchandiser
Gross Profit Per Oil Change	$8.40	$11.04
Changes Per Hour	3	3
Gross Profit Per Hour	$25.20	$33.12
Annual Technician Gross Profit	$50,400	$66,240
Number of Shop Technicians	8	8
Total Shop Gross Profit	**$403,200**	**$529,920**

$125,000 in additional profit per year, taken over ten years, totals $1.25 million in extra return. This gross profit margin argument is difficult to win with a dealership technician and impossible to contemplate with the customer. Would you ever tolerate; "In order for the dealership to have the same profit margin as Jiffy Lube, we will have to charge you $30 more per hour." Sure. It's even worse with a banker. They know by comparison, dealerships are riskier bets than quick lubes. But you need dealerships to fix the stuff nobody else will fool with. So that leaves the automakers with some decisions to make.

The Automakers Idea On How To Fix Things
(Without Costing Them a Dime)

Manufacturers cajole dealers to recruit, hire, and train $12 per hour technicians for quick service work. They can perform virtually all the mileage services the individual automakers recommend, except perhaps timing belts. However, in doing so, the gravy jobs are denied to the more highly-skilled and highly-compensated techs. This policy creates the greatest uproars during weeks when techs are being barbecued by those difficult warranty diagnostic issues that keep them from producing a decent paycheck. Certifications get techs hired at the hourly rate they want. Gravy work gets them the paycheck they need. Dealers cannot have their cake and eat it too. Meaning, they cannot have highly-skilled technicians sitting around for free, waiting for tough factory type jobs, while all the easy jobs go to lower-priced technicians. In this way, service profitability continues to be difficult in the dealership game. The talented guys must be kept happy so they are available to do the tough diagnostic and repair work customers demand.

The whole system cheats dealerships out of some of the best and often critical profit opportunities and cheats customers out of a better supply of service technicians to work on their vehicles. And the automakers, with their discounted labor time-guides and discounted warranty parts markups, don't help matters. Nobody wants to work on your tough diagnostic and repair problems, because there is no money in it. The automakers just don't pay, preferring instead to audit and charge back what they have already funded their dealers.

Thirteen

Why Automakers Could Never Sell You a Car

...and Why You Would Never Want Them To

*"Most people spend more time
and energy going around problems
than in trying to solve them"*

—HENRY FORD
Founder of Ford Motor Co. & Innovator of
Assembly-Line Manufacturing (1863–1947)

nstead of solving these obvious flaws in their policies and keeping the American consumer happy in their dealerships, manufacturers such as General Motors and Chrysler have a history of manipulating and overhauling their dealer networks. Time and time again, they buy out some, target others for extinction, and glorify others with huge cash investments—free money—as incentive to go out on a limb and build a gargantuan facility. If a factory program hurts dealers, or even puts them out of business, the manufacturer's attitude is they will just get someone else to represent the area.

Automakers have no blessed idea how a dealer does what he does, but most are eager to tell them how to do things. Peter Fitzpatrick, a former service manager and remaining friend of mine was fond of the expression; "You can either tell me *what* you want done or *how* you want me to do it—but not both." The factory does both. Every tier of their management model specializes in directing both the "whats" and "hows" of dealer practices. No small feat, considering virtually none of them ever actually worked in a dealership; and neither sold nor repaired cars.

District managers see to it dealers take as much product as possible, helping them out of procedural snags and jams. Zone managers see that it is done by expending a minimal amount of factory resources. National managers set policy and budgets. But virtually none of them know how to run stores. They have never done so.

Nonetheless, they are steadfast in their insistence that they know best. In addition to dealing with factory folks most of my life and sharing similar stories with other dealers throughout my career, I also attended one of their training academies. I didn't learn much there about selling cars or operating dealerships. But I did learn the roots of the automaker's arrogant aloofness.

Chevrolet Dealership Management School

Meet the Chevrolet Dealership Management School on Van Dyke Parkway in Warren, Michigan. Founded as "Dealer's Son's School," renamed "Dealer's Son's and Daughter's School," and finally "Dealership Management School." Students included mostly dealer's kids, some in-laws, and a dealer or two. Most of the students were serious about making a career in the business. Others lacked sobriety. One dealer's son was kicked out for blowing off classes or coming in late. He'd head across the border to Windsor, Canada, get hammered in the bars and fail to wake up on time for class. Rumor had it, his dad's zone manager was contacted. Not a good thing those days in Chevrolet's world.

Attendance might have been important to the factory, but it was really a superfluous issue. There was very little learning going on there at all. Tim Diese gave a great lecture on used vehicle reconditioning. Tim taught us that an open can of coffee grounds with a slice or two of fresh apple can drive most smells out of a used car. Nat Shulman, who had sold his dealership to his son Scott and written a book about it, gave a great lecture. He helped me better understand my dad and our relationship. Nat just passed away. God rest his soul. He was a tremendous sage.

Tom Stuker lectured on phone skills. At the time, there was no internet, so potential customers would call dealership after dealership to get information on a given dealer's inventory. They had questions and requests of color, interior and "your lowest selling price." Tom thought a lot about handling these phone questions and still writes call-guides or scripts for dealer employees to use when a potential customer calls in. Prior to Tom, consumers calling dealerships with questions were likely to hear: "I'm not at my desk right now ... I'm not allowed to quote prices over the phone ... I have six *available* like that." (Translation: I will order one from the factory or swap one in from another dealer)

Tom pioneered the idea of a designated "Call-Room." He advocated that these be set up in every dealership, at least those that wanted to be competitive and increase sales. This concept was and is sound and ultimately developed into the "Business Development Center," as customer database technology expanded. This lecture was an opportunity for him to pick up some consulting work by setting up those rooms for the students' dealerships.

He became extremely aggravated with me when I pressed him. I wanted to know how to handle the customer who would not come into the dealership unless we quoted a price over the phone. Instead of giving me the answers (which I am sure he is able to provide at this point in his success story) he said; "Who are you, Dobie Gillis? You know, you are never going to be successful in this business because you are focused on fiction instead of reality."

Well, in my world, people wanted information. They were tired of going back and forth between the five same-make Chevrolet dealers, within a 45-minute driving radius, to beat their last offer. That's the success of the internet, isn't it? People want information and they want it fast.

Other than that little embarrassing incident, Stuker was terrific
and scared the pants off the factory guy in charge who "found the language bordering on coercive." And for the record, I did sort of look like
Dobie Gillis, or at least my hair did. Today, I would trade the hair I
had twenty years ago for all the insults a guy like Stuker might hurl.

Chevrolet also brought in this Ph.D. Psycho-something-or-other
guy, who wanted us to unify in a consciousness of "we could all compete as dealers, get along and make money, if we were tuned to the idea
of sharing." Then we meditated on it. Literally, lights off and meditat-
ing on the floor. The last time I had done this was naptime at nursery
school when my mom packed me a blankie. I have to say, as an adult, it
was very relaxing, but I am not sure it cured me from the desire to tear
my competitors' heads off when competing for customers.

Afterward, we ran a mock computer simulation where we made
dealership financial decisions and punched them into a computer
model. The computer scored our every move in play dollars. We had
received absolutely no financial statement training whatsoever, mind
you. This was surprising, being in the educational care of the folks who
designed that statement. They also wrote their own factory accounting manual, which was never mentioned or referred to even once. But
we were to nonetheless awaken from our meditative states to play the
game: Make the Most Net Profit.

The winning team had decided to take out a capital loan, purchase and stock a massive amount of parts, and launch a wholesale
parts business. The simulator loved the team with big enough ideas to
borrow money and sink it into factory inventory like drunken sailors.
Consequently, the software rewarded them with a wad of parts sales
and associated net profit to go with it, and they won. If that were the
lesson—to run a better parts operation—we could have better learned
from a dealership parts guru. However, parts department management
was not the point. The point was; if you buy lots of factory stuff—no
matter what leverage or risk might be required—you win.

Classmates of mine theorized that the factory wanted us
numbed and dumbed-down, thus explaining why we had no

financial training whatsoever. The argument makes sense. If we looked at things like informed businesspeople, we'd be more likely to become critical of factory sponsored programs. The dealer staying stupid aids the automaker. Of course, stupidity really doesn't help anybody; it just undermines everyone's success—in the real world at least.

A fine education is available for prospective car dealers and for that matter, factory employees. Unfortunately, such tutelage may never come from automakers. How can they teach what they neither know nor understand? So my father sponsored me through another school—designed, developed, and administrated by car dealers.

NADA Dealer Candidate Academy

My first session of NADA Dealership Candidate Academy (DCA) occurred *after* my first session with the Chevrolet folks. 1989 was a very busy travel year for me. In addition to the pair of two-week sessions in Warren, Michigan at the factory, I traveled to six different U.S. cities for one-week sessions to study with the DCA. The program was run by dealers, for dealers, so they didn't mess around with factory politics or meditation gurus. We were there to work and learn.

The first DCA session required six weeks of prior home study preparation. We were tasked with filling out a workbook with hundreds of equations pertinent to the financial statement. They had a unique way of teaching the math, by utilizing cellular addresses similar to what you would find on an excel spreadsheet: "page 4, column 3, line 68 divided by page 3, column 6, line 23 = Hours Sold per Customer Service Repair Order," for example. We would look at this stuff and analyze it until we went cross-eyed. Many DCA days, like the car business itself, involved fourteen hours of headache-generating work. A grind customarily followed by two hours of drinking it away in the hotel bar.

Each department of the dealership was covered in the first five DCA sessions. Six weeks of in-department study, report, and workbook exercises were followed by a week of classroom hammering. It was really boot camp for car dealers. I often came home exhausted and completely burned out on the business. I didn't want to even ride home from the airport in a car, much less talk about cars or the business itself for several days following.

However, there was a method to the DCA madness. Students learned the financial guts of the business and how to develop work stamina. The sixth and final session required teams of five to analyze the complete financial performance of a mock dealership, project and forecast its future performance, based on specific operational plans, and structure a purchase and sale of the store. This was something I would use in my career several times over; in purchasing, constructing, and operating six franchised auto dealerships and three franchised motorcycle dealerships. It proved to be well worth the temporary burnout. After all, I could always return to Warren, Michigan and take another meditative nap if I needed to relax!

The dichotomy of training between these two dealership-management schools still bakes my noodle to this day. It is inexplicable and amazing how truly out of touch automakers are with what goes on inside their dealerships. And if they are unaware of what goes on at all the customer touch-points, how can they ever help dealers sell you things and satisfy you? In that vein, there are many ex-factory managers who have made great dealers, by putting themselves through the same rigmarole that I have. But in my entire adult life and most of my childhood, I can only recall two former dealership guys who went to work for an automaker. This is not a point made about competence or intelligence, but rather experience, perspective, and understanding.

How the Automakers "Train" Their Employees to Treat Customers

I don't know how to run a plant, but I do know how to get along with car dealers by understanding their challenges, stresses, pressure and breaking points. My point is moot, however, because automakers have no one working for them—in any capacity whatsoever—who understands their dealers' point of view. How many automaker board members are former car dealers? I am not speaking of dealer advisory boards, I'm talking about dealers having a seat on the board of directors of their manufacturing, wholesale operations and captive financial arms. There are none.

Consequently, no one with any consumer experience is teaching front-line managers what you, the customer, needs. By front-line, I am talking about factory district sales and service managers (DMs). During my tenure owning dealerships, I found most of them were between the ages of 23–33. How many dealers are within that age range? Not many. Most of my factory representatives were just kids who really knew nothing about the car business. But they drank the "automaker failure is due to the dealers," Kool-Aid mixed up by their bosses. Consequently DMs often come into dealerships expecting dealers to be difficult, demanding, unappreciative, spoiled brats. They often appear frustrated and aloof, becoming vindictive in defense of the programs their boss requires them to sell.

The highest percentages of arrogance, in my personal experience, were at GM followed by Honda. The behavior of Honda's employees is similar to GM's during the waning days of their former glory. Not the way to either treat a customer or teach him how to treat *his* customers. Kia has the most polite sales and service organizations in the business, as far as I am concerned. While it is unfair to cast all factory-to-dealer contact managers in either light, automakers have a real problem here. Despite some that were pleasant, many were arrogant. I am not talking about minor philosophical disagreements, either. I am talking about an either "you do this or else" attitude.

Very few factory programs stick, because they are devised in boardrooms a billion miles away from dealer retailers and retail customers. In addition, it seems the initiatives that work the best are pulled off the table the fastest. It's the job of the DMs to sell the dealer cars, keep their warranty costs down, and get dealers to take inventory.

Of course, a major focus on their plate is dealer sign-ups for new executive-inspired programs.

Factory middle-management doesn't get it either. Why should they? Factory middle-management is made up of former DMs somebody promoted. Zone managers fill DMs heads with expectations and attitudes about every dealer in their district. Their bosses before them did the same. Since DMs do not know enough to object, they go out and do what DMs do. Only most of them swing with a swagger of attitude to beat the band. And guess what? They eventually get promoted. Next thing you know, they've got a big job with the automaker, overseeing the next generation of DM minions.

Today, we have two or three management tiers of uneducated factory policy makers driving the industry off a cliff, dealers first. If automakers would just send these folks out for some education before they become the next generation of power brokers, we would be looking at better ideas that sell more cars. Instead, manufacturers rely on the detachment of their senior management—raised in this culture I am describing—to come up with the ideas. Just like their bosses before them, they hold the DM kids responsible for jamming those ideas down car dealers' throats.

DM kids just hang in there waiting for the day when they can move up the ladder. At that point, they won't have to take so much guff from dealers while implementing their boss' programs. They know full well how their employers' corporate politics work. They aspire, to one day "earn" a promotion where they get to create programs in a vacuum and pass them down the line for DMs to jam into the dealer network. They figure that this is being promoted to a nirvana job; hiding behind a desk, setting policy, enjoying the immunity afforded their bosses before them.

This remains a generational curse that management passes on as corporate culture and lineage. A modus operandi consisting of this type of attitude leads to decisions with no accountability. Decisions made without accountability is the definition of immunity. Immunity is what has the automakers in so much trouble. They have no experience in automotive retail. They don't like or respect most people in automotive retail. So is it any wonder they are apt to blame retailers undeservedly for many situations created at their level? Is it any wonder they make decisions that actually *prevent* their dealers from selling cars and satisfying customers? To make matters worse, sometimes, they let their good employees get away.

Kevin Timmerman, my first Pontiac Service DM, was brilliant at his job. He wasn't the guy who would *get* you an answer to your question; he was the guy who always *knew* the answer to your question—a rare find for General Motors. However, he was not a schmoozer and thus not a good candidate for promotion. He left GM to teach at a technical college. The factory lost a good guy in Kevin.

Conversely, there was an employee working out of the zone office referred to as "Delco Doug." This guy's sole responsibility was to stroll into dealerships unannounced and demand an audience with the dealer in order to pitch factory CD players. His air and presentation were extremely condescending and dealers really didn't like him, so Doug and his agenda were the furthest thing from their minds at ordering time. It was a cakewalk job for an obnoxious person who somebody at the factory favored.

The Good Ones: A Quarter-Century of Notable Exceptions

I've had district sales, service and parts managers who were awful and I won't name them here. I've had some fantastic ones too. One great example is Michael Carr from Kia, who moved on to the top sales management job at Subaru of New England—a regional Subaru distributorship owned by the Boch family. Ken Domingues of Kia, is a tremendously talented district service and parts manager, who demonstrates a high level of experience, competence and understanding. Another good example is Don Paparella from Pontiac, who was hired by Honda after they asked me for a referral on a great district sales manager. I can't forget Robin Sanders of Pontiac, who moved on to a big job at the Saturn division, and Regis Buckley from Chevrolet, a former mascot at Michigan State University and a dynamite DM who helped us out of all kinds of situations.

There are a number of mid-level and upper-level managers I have personally enjoyed working with also, including; Tim Maloney, Elliott Eichenholz, Jim Vranich, Brian Smith, Wayne Englehardt, Troy Irrer, Barry Alick, Carlos Latour, Scott Bell, Peter Delvecchio, and Mark LaNeve of GM. Jack Vossenberg, Michael Tocci, Randy Bube, Scott Pickard, Dick Macedo, B.M. Ahn, and Peter Butterfield of Kia, and, Jim Sweeting, Mark Cronin, Jim Foley, Dick Szamborski and Dick Colliver of Honda. Not that we always agreed on every issue, but that we could *respectfully* and *mutually* agree to disagree.

I've seen them come and go by quitting, promotion or transfer. But in my entire career, terrific or deplorable, I've seen only Kia fire and replace its managers at any level. My wife, Lauri, a former General Motors DM says; "GM deserves exactly what they get. Even today (they are) not accountable." While all automakers differ somewhat in personality, they are all blood-brothers in some respects—wandering together down the road less-traveled by other industries.

Fourteen

The People You Deal with at the Dealership

... The Good, The Bad, and The Ugly

"No change of circumstances can repair a defect of character."

—RALPH WALDO EMERSON
Poet, Lecturer, and Essayist (1803–1882)

Employees are second on the list of car dealers' bosses. Next to a game-changing twist by the factory, no one else can influence a car dealership's success or failure so quickly. Some dealers kid themselves into thinking they have control over their employees. Others are blessed to do business in areas of the country retaining a few more Protestant work ethic values. You know the ones I mean. Putting current definitions of political incorrectness aside, I am talking about the the hard work that built our nation. I am talking about employees who put their fiduciary duties *first* in their decision making process. But the sad truth is that few dealership employees operate this way.

The Good

There is a core group of extremely conscientious employees in most every dealership. Some are ardently loyal and would no more steal from their own mother than hurt their dealer. The common trait among these individuals is *great character*. Great character can be stretched, challenged and leveraged to accomplish amazing things. Great character cannot be taught or learned, however. It is either possessed innately, or forever elusive to an individual. Great character is easy to work with. Conversely, those employees lacking great character require too much supervision, too much prodding, and are too quick with performance excuses.

Dealers must start with character and develop from there. Talent is second. Character without talent is not very profitable, mind you. But talent without character is an accident waiting to happen. Some of my finest general managers, such as Robert Baker, for example, began as lot attendants with either my father or me. They didn't have M.B.A.s, but they did have Ph.D.s: Poor, Hungry and Determined. And they leveraged these qualities for personal growth, income and accomplishment. I have also employed some notorious cats who leveraged personal greed to cheat and steal from my customers, my employees, and my company. This doesn't make me special. Every dealer I know has gone through similar issues to a greater or lesser degree.

Part of the problem stems from a lack of dealership hiring standards. This is to say that virtually anyone can get a job in a car dealer's showroom. The car business is the last bastion of opportunity for someone with little or no formal education and even no proof of identification. With these qualifications, he or she could still land a potential $100,000 per year job, in virtually any city in America within a 24 hour period.

Regardless of an individual dealer's hiring standards there is an extreme lack of character in the car business gene-pool of potential hires. Why? Do you know anybody raising a child today, hoping he or she will land a fantastic career in the car business? I don't either, except parents who are already car dealers. This is what makes dealership ownership and operation such a generational business, from father or mother to son or daughter.

Aside from the family working at the store, everyone else just landed at their first car dealership job on a "try." They didn't plan to get there, like a teacher, vocational tradesman, or legal or medical professional. Instead, dealers seem to attract the situationally challenged individuals ranging from those experiencing a layoff in an unrelated industry to others running from out-of-state arrest warrants.

Most folks who have great character maintain solid family lives. They demonstrate both loyalty and faithfulness in the household, which rarely morphs or changes in the workplace. Family people don't want to be away from their families working sixty to seventy hours per week, unless it reconciles with their value system. This means providing for their family in a big way: nice house, nice vacations, great educations, and some toys to enjoy together during time off. Quality of life and plans for the future trump quantity of time with spouse and children.

People that have disasters for family lives are willing to work any hours provided the money is good. They require less of it, however, because less is shared with others. Outside of personal substance or gambling addictions and mandatory child-support payments . . . Well, you get the picture.

These supply and demand dynamics in competition for the holy grail of simultaneous talent *and* character; take dealership personnel costs north to points of foolishness. A dealer spends roughly half of his gross profit on people. This figure does not include commissions to salespeople or technicians' pay. In many markets, dealership employees (particularly salespeople) can and do run no more than a quarter-mile up the street, gaining employment at another dealership 24 hours *before* leaving their old job. How does a dealer ever make change happen in his business operating in this kind of environment? The dealer up the street is willing to put up an extra buck or more shenanigans or whatever. Nonetheless, we all pick the kitchen we are in and the heat that comes along with it.

The Bad

Before I became dealer at Ragsdale-Fuller Pontiac Cadillac in 1996, I found myself in need of a finance manager (also referred to as a business manager in Jack and Jill's story). We put the word out and ran an ad in the city newspaper. In came this cat, dressed to the nines—right down to his alligator loafers. And here was his story:

He was married to a local police chief's daughter and was moving back into the area because of her corporate job relocation. Finance managers are responsible for placing consumer auto loans with banks for a profit as well as selling optional mechanical repair insurance and other products at a profit. He had all the right answers to all the right questions. He was happy with the pay plan being offered. If ever there was a perfect fit for this position, I was positive he was it. A consultant named Phil Lavoie, of Dealership Management Associates, had helped me write the ad and sat in on the interview. We both concurred on hiring him pending reference checks.

When I got to the first reference, things checked out. The general manager told me his performance was great, but he had left in a hurry. This, of course, was understandable—especially in light of his wife's job relocation. However, before I hung up the phone, I asked a simple, but powerful question; "Is there anyone else you would recommend I talk to, before making my final decision?" This single inquisition gains instant access to references whom candidates neglect to put on their resumes—people they presumably prefer you not speak with. If they did, I reckon they would have included their name on the list.

"You should call So and So," he said.

So I called Mr. So and So. This gentleman's assessment of my candidate was not so flattering. Apparently, Mr. So and So was a dealer himself. Upon my candidate's speedy departure from his business, the dealer found a number of executed extended service insurance contracts stuffed in the finance office desk. This was the second example of a quick departure by my candidate; this time, not due to his wife's job relocation, but in the wake of a larceny scam frosted with insurance fraud.

Customers—mostly immigrants suffering with language barrier issues—had paid cash for these insurance policies and received an invalid receipt generated out of a bogus receipt book. The con was to sell the policy, pocket the cash, give the customer a dummy receipt and copy of the contract, but never place the policy with the carrier. Instead, he just pocketed the money and left the dealer with a huge insurance liability.

I now understood why my slick con artist applicant moved around so quickly in those expensive alligator loafers. The rest of his story about his wife being the daughter of a local police chief was all true. If I had stuck to the references listed on his resume, I would have probably found myself in the same shape as the last two dealers he shafted. These types of scams take a while to turn up, but when they do, they blow big.

We chose someone else for the position. He worked for me for nine years as a finance manager. His numbers were below standard, but he always took care of my customers. Today, he is a partner in an extended service contract insurance agency and doing very well. No doubt, as a result of having great character.

The trade-off here was enormous. The con man candidate was capable of tremendous numbers. Those dollars would have changed the entire financial picture of a small store like mine. We were doing about 800 units per year. A difference of just $300 profit per vehicle— through increased product sales—would have brought an additional $200,000 per year to the bottom line. We were only making about $75,000 annually at the time.

In one sense, the finance manager I chose over the con artist cost the company $1.5 million over his nine year tenure. But my customers were happy. Who knows how many repeat buyers and loyal service customers the dealership gained because of the straight dealings he consistently commanded out of his office? Could we have hired the stud and put tight controls in place in order to monitor theft? Sure. Do I have eyes in the back of my head? Nope.

For the record, the stud ended up having a couple brief stints at local dealerships going through ownership changes and was in the finance office at a local boat dealership before it went out of business. That was the last I heard of him.

There is one outstanding common principle to hiring experienced individuals from the competition: They *always* go out the way they came in! If they came in with addictions to drugs, alcohol, gambling or women, chances sadly are that they will most probably leave with those conditions as well. If they left their last post in a cloud of unethical or questionable circumstances, they will always leave the next dealer—in the same manner—or perhaps even worse.

However, previous employer info isn't always easy to come by. In reviewing the finer points of reference checking, sometimes even getting a current reference from a currently-employed applicant proves impossible. They haven't left their current job yet, but are happy to move on to the next dealer's employment on one condition; the new dealership accepts the applicant's testimony that he is being deprived, cheated, or somehow abused by his current employer. "I can no longer tolerate working under those conditions, but you can't verify my story without getting me fired," is a common interview ice-breaker in the automobile business.

Sometimes this is the case. Just as there are a thousand ways for an employee to rip off a dealership, there are a thousand more ways some dealers cheat their employees out of duly earned pay. A close competitor was famous for jacking with commissioned salespersons' pay by lowering the internal value of customers' trade-ins, after the deal and delivery were made. This practice proved inconsequential to retail customers. Their deal didn't change a lick. Instead, it was an internal bookkeeping method designed to lower the profits, along with salesperson commissions. Trimming each car deal's expenses by an average of a hundred dollars each would increase this dealer's net profit by six figures per year. So when I had an applicant who was leaving that dealership, but hadn't yet quit, I was more inclined to buy the story.

In the Northeast, roughly half of all dealers pay salary as some component of their salesperson's compensation plan. This practice is less in vogue and downright frowned upon in many other U.S. car markets. The preponderance of dealers offering salespeople salaries are typically struggling for profitability while representing unfashionable brands. Franchised dealerships representing makes that are out of the pop culture find floor traffic tough to come by. Consequently, most salespeople with any kind of talent will only come aboard for "the push the noodle up a hill with a chopstick party" if they have a sufficient safety net. This requires guaranteed income and/or salary.

Eating Snake With A Chilled Merlot

My wife Lauri and I attempted to recruit a pair of salespeople from a large Toyota dealer in our market and cajole them into joining our Pontiac-Cadillac store. Actually, we wanted just one of the guys, but it was made clear to us that they came as a duo or not at all. We rented a limousine, picking both candidates up at their separate residences— along with their girlfriends—and headed off to the finest restaurant in the city.

Lauri asked some questions of our server about their filet mignon. One of the girlfriends perked up and inquired; "Oh, what is that?"

The other responded with conviction; "It is the best part of the steak."

"Snake . . . I've never eaten snake. Is it good?" She asked.

"Yes. I like it very much."

Lauri intervened in an attempt to diffuse the potentially embarrassing exchange, before the conversation dilapidated further.

"Yuck. I think I'll stick with chicken," she surrendered—with an abrupt change of subject—ordering a *chilled* Merlot to wash her meal down.

Our $700 evening culminated in the pairs' demand for $150,000 in guaranteed annual compensation each. I politely declined. They explained they were earning somewhere in that range at their current dealership and would need this kind of safety net in order to jump that ship and come aboard ours. No matter. They were still unaffordable.

I wondered what they did with that kind of money. Certainly taking their companions out for fine dining experiences wasn't among their social priorities. What kind of conversation would have ensued if my wife ordered a rib-eye? The same young lady called me late one night, some months later offering her boyfriend's employment services at a bargain price if I was willing to bail him out of jail on a stalking charge. Apparently there was some misunderstanding when he followed a terrified ex-girlfriend into a police station parking lot in violation of a restraining order.

The Roving Sage: Voted Most Likely To Wear Wide Ties And White Shoes

Foodies, stalkers, or not—talented salespeople would rather bag $400 per car in commissions than be guaranteed a $400 per week salary in a dead store. Of notable and unworthy exception, however, is the Roving Sage. Offering little more than inordinate pride and a calico history of past accomplishments on which he expects to retire. Today he is nothing more a quintessential order-taker. When this applicant enters the dealership, Bruce Springsteen's *Glory Days* spontaneously erupts from the paging system. He was the showroom equivalent of Larry Bird during the days of 75% domestic market share. The fact that customers had fewer choices, lower expectations, and less financial issues at the time doesn't hurt the Roving Sage's Hall of Fame status either.

Salary is a key for him, as well as management's willingness to pay him extra for a performance at or below national average. However, because many dealers are better at sticking their heads in the sand than their upside-down customers so they hire the Roving Sage expecting incremental gains in business from his "loyal" customer following. Dealers generally fail to acknowledge that he is also the guy holding board meetings, behind the dumpster, with the balance of their sales staff. This place is where more than "just" cancer of the lungs is spread. If only our Superstar of Yesteryear spent half as much time and energy contacting his "loyal" customer base as he does ratting out our otherwise hopeful sales department, we might have something. Perhaps the compensation plan and hire might be worth the suitcase of aggravation accompanying him from job to job.

Most times however, he leaves the way he came in, but only after destroying the morale of otherwise great employees. If possible, he will drag some young hopeful talent from the store, now infected by his vagabond rants, and seeking greener pastures on the other side of the fence.

In the worst, but not so uncommon cases, Rovers depart in the wake of costly sexual harassment allegations. These guys view the office behavior in episodes of *Mad Men* as training films. "Honey", "Baby", and other nomenclature of the like are their lexicon of preference, while swatting an unsuspecting receptionist in the buttocks.

The Ugly

When a dealer accepts an applicant at a senior management level position from the competition, you can bet your boots he is in for an almost complete turnover of sales management and salespeople. And accompanying him will be any number of the above Hodge-podge-lodge cast of characters. This is a foregone outcome, unless the senior manager has either been ineffective to work for in the past, or is relocating from a great geographic distance.

When hiring a local manager from a local competitor, with a track record of results, dealers anticipate him bringing his loyal "team" with him, the operative word being "his." This team could more aptly be referred to as a band of gypsies, and, I mean no disrespect to gypsies. They travel in packs, each loyal to the leader who brings them from fresh kill to carrion.

It is very tempting for dealers to bring someone like this into their organization. Sometimes, sheer survival requires instant performance turnarounds in order to avoid dire financial consequences. Desperate times call for desperate measures. Many of these folks are scary talented. Most lack great character or any character at all for that matter. I have hired folks like these on more than one occasion and paid the price for it later on. Why? They *always* go out the way they came in.

In the case of the pack—a rag-tag community of Barbary Coast emigres—any procedural or policy change contemplated by the dealer is subject to their complete buy-in. By default, this buy-in is controlled, not by the dealer, but by the pack leader. In this way, the dealership is hijacked by the pack and their leader's prurient self-interests, rather than under the control of the dealer principal. WIIFM, is their favorite radio station: What's In It For Me? Since they are not planning on retiring there, or getting a Rolex for a career of unbroken service, no decision or action is ever executed for the common good. Every move they make is motivated by temporary gratification, no matter what the damage to the company, fellow employees or customers.

The strategy for setting up camp is simple and highly effective. Put the pack in place by blowing out long-term loyal employees. Then work both ends against the middle. He will tell the dealer what he wants to hear, by agreeing to decisions behind closed doors, then go the other way in front of his pack. "You know I wouldn't do this to you myself, but _____ (fill in the blank) is making me do it." A constant undercurrent of control is maintained by the pack leader in this way. Everyone in his circle, beginning with him, is always looking for the BBD; Bigger-Better-Deal. It is his charge to perpetually convince those around him, that he is their equivalent of Moses—exclusively trusted to lead them to the promised land. However, nobody is sticking around for forty years, never mind forty minutes, if there is a BBD to be had somewhere else.

Financial reporting must be kept separate from the control of the pack leader. He may *review* financial reports, but not *create* them. He may have some of his people working in the office, but the pack leader must not fill the office manager or controller positions. Folks ardently loyal to the dealer—and the dealer only—must hold these positions. A dealer may make that trade-off of character for results on the sales floor and pay for it later. However, if his financial chief lacks character, he may pay for it with the loss of his whole business.

Pack leaders are the Devil's pawns. When one dances with them, he takes his business (and his sanity) into the nether regions of hell. I can smell these cats a mile away. Since you can never change the spots on a leopard, they must be replaced with men and women of integrity as soon as practical, even if this requires the changeover of key employees who the pack leader rolled into town with. Far better to deal with them on one's own clock, than wake-up to an ill-timed emergency: when the dealership has been emptied of employees, cash, contracts, customer and vendor lists, financial data and merchandise—literally overnight.

My son once asked me, "How do you know when someone is a good person?"

I answered, "Good people have a conscience."

He responded, "How can you tell if someone has a conscience?"

I replied, "When they do something they shouldn't, they are bothered about it."

The main ingredient for great character is integrity. Integrity means doing the right thing even when no one is looking. People without a conscience have no compunction about doing whatever they wish when no one is looking. Even when caught red-handed, they manufacture a litany of excuses—or out and out lie—in order to justify their actions.

My sister, Kimberly Ragsdale Kennedy, is highly educated and extremely accomplished professional, with a Master's Degree in Total

Quality Management (TQM). As I grew my dealership group from three to six stores, I lured her away from a premier national insurance company in order to engineer and document best practices for our workforce. Ultimately, she returned to the insurance industry shaking her head at the automobile business and its employees. "You just can never have a conversation and turn your back expecting something to get done," she said. "It's like herding cats."

Fifteen

Where Dealers Get the Cash to Stock All Those Cars

... and It's Not From Making Money on You

"A bank is a place that will lend you money
if you can prove that you don't need it."

—BOB HOPE
Comedian & U.S. Honorary Military Veteran
(1903–2003)

Similar to most small businesses, dealerships do not have millions of dollars in cash to pay up front for their entire vehicle inventory. Therefore, with few exceptions, dealers rely on banks to supply these inventory lines of credit. Dealer floorplan is a term used to describe this credit arrangement. The bank funds the factory for cars it builds via a dealer floorplan line, often as soon as those freshly built vehicles are loaded onto the truck for dealer delivery.

Automakers achieve positive cash flow by delivering to and immediately receiving cash from their dealers in this manner. Quick math says a car dealer selling seventy-five new vehicles per month and carrying a sixty day (two-month) supply of cars would be stocking approximately 150 units. If each of these vehicles cost the dealer an average of $20,000, he would have to borrow $3 million from his floorplan lender in order to meet his stocking requirements.

The business of floorplan financing is offered by few banks and watched like a hawk by those that do. You see, the only real security the bank has, when investing in dealer inventory, is that inventory itself. Of course, they also list a dealer's parts inventories, computers, tools, and furniture as additional collateral. Additionally, however, they get personal. Meaning, they require the personal guarantee of any individual owning 10% or more of the franchise contract.

Sometimes, banks even seek non-related, 0% ownership individuals as third-party personal guarantors. Consequently, if a dealership goes down, a lot of folks go down with it. But despite having everything to repossess—from the dealer's uncle's house to the junior partner's coffee table—banks remain nervous as sinners in church about providing floorplan financing to dealers.

Let me give you an example from my personal experience. In August 2002, I took out a $5.85 million loan to purchase the remaining shares of our Chevrolet and Kia dealerships, as well as the real estate, from my family. It was a non-traditional note, with virtually no ability to prepay. The lender had used the investments of secured bondholders, as their capital mechanism, to loan me this kind of money. This meant I was stuck with my lender for 15 years, regardless of any other ideas I might want to exercise during that time. The mortgage contract specified; I could not sell the properties, close the dealerships, move the franchises, or refinance any of the above with another lender. These were onerous stipulations, since the dealerships sat some 45 minutes apart, in two very different markets, representing two very different products. My monthly mortgage payment was $63,000, at an interest rate that was 400 basis points (4 APR percentage points) above the market. This was required to satisfy my family's interests so I agreed to the terms.

The dealership's floorplan arrangements were with another bank altogether: Citizen's Bank owned by the Royal Bank of Scotland (RBS). Citizen's kept taking runs at me to switch my mortgage financing over to them. Their motivation was to gain greater equity in the overall deal, by securing the real estate as additional collateral. This was not possible for them to accomplish as long as the mortgage was held by these other bondholders. The proposed change would have been better for my companies as well, because the new interest rate Citizen's offered was significantly lower.

My current mortgage lender miraculously agreed to let me out of the deal. The bondholders were willing to waive over $1.2 million in interest penalties that would have been due upon prepayment of the loan. They had performed more recent appraisals and felt as though I now owed too much on the real estate, or was upside-down in my real estate. Consequently, they were happy to see me go away, preferring instead to invest their money outside of commercial real estate. Ironic, isn't it? After helping my customers go further upside-down in car loans all those years, now I was upside-down in my mortgage.

It looked like we were all going to come out of this one happy. My old lender could get rid of me and reinvest in other markets. Citizen's Bank was going to pick up more security in my dealerships as well as make more interest from me by loaning the mortgage money. And my companies were going to pay a lower interest rate with more flexibility to prepay or refinance the properties down the road.

At the last minute, however, Citizen's decided to require a personal guarantee from my father in order to write the new mortgage. This meant they would give me the loan, but if I failed to pay it back, my father and mother would have to pick up the tab. Neither my father, nor my mother had owned even one share of my companies in the last five years. Nonetheless, the bank wanted the security in having them guarantee the note. I refused to put my parents in that situation. Consequently, Citizen's refused to honor the deal. The bondholders at the mortgage lender took the deal off the table, and we all went our merry or not so merry ways.

It was Citizen's idea to offer this new deal in the first place. As my floorplan source, they already knew everything about me and my companies. If I lacked ample professional and personal assets for a loan approval, why did they offer me an additional $4.5 million in loans?

A New Order Lower Than Whale S#!T:
Bankers, Lawyers, Politicians, Car Salesmen

Why no mention of additional collateral requirements until the very last minute? The profitability of the dealerships had remained consistent throughout the application process. There were no new facets of the deal for them to consider. Nothing remotely material had changed.

Citizen's simply banked (pun intended) on me with providing them with whatever they wanted in order to take advantage of $1.2 million in interest penalty forbearance by my bondholders. They knew that if the new mortgage didn't close, the bondholders would be upset and put those penalties back on the table. They saw this as an opportunity to squeeze and leverage me to get what they wanted. Most bankers are opportunists. They were no different.

This eleventh-hour wrangling by Citizen's not only cost me thousands of dollars in needless appraisal fees, but also angered the mortgage bondholders. Citizen's, who wanted more of me than the $60,000 in floorplan interest they collected from my businesses each month, ended up costing me almost $750,000 in penalties, when I later paid off the bondholder note. Banks pull this stuff all the time. Some are worse than others. But certainly, Citizen's and the RBS are among the nastiest—charging some dealers thousands of dollars in quarterly administrative paperwork fees—just to keep their floorplan lines open. Disgusting.

Why are floorplan lenders so predatory and skittish? Well, simply put, if a dealer delivers the cars to customers but fails to pay off the bank as they do so, the bank can find itself millions of dollars short. Imagine a dealer delivering 100 cars this way and failing to pay off the bank as he went. At an average of $20,000 apiece, that dealer could fall behind by two million dollars in just four weeks' time! The cars are gone, the floorplan lenders collateral security is gone, and the money to satisfy their note is nowhere to be found.

In addition to demanding everything including a dealer's kitchen sink for collateral, floorplan lenders are moving more towards a position of refusing floorplan loans unless they also hold the mortgage on the dealer's facility. A dealers' ability to borrow money and function grows less and less potent during weak commercial real estate markets. Most of the time, for liability and tax purposes, dealers form separate corporate or partnership entities to own their real estate. This enables them to shield their property from angry or dishonest employees, customers and banks.

However, wherever potential bank losses may loom, lenders want personal assets they can grab in case business goes south and the bills cannot be paid. Consequently, banks try to tie in the shareholders or partners who own the real estate into their floorplan collateral. Meaning, if a dealership doesn't pay off floorplan lines as they deliver cars, the bank can repossess the real estate. In order to do this, they must carry the mortgage and ensure the real estate owners are listed as guarantors in the floorplan agreement. As the lenders tighten, the guarantor requirements go up. If not met, the bank simply terminates their floorplan arrangements with the dealer. Meaning, dealers can no longer buy cars from the factory or auction. They cannot even afford to take trade-ins.

No Inventory = No Sales = No Income = No Dealership

But the fun doesn't stop there! Banks also discontinue approving customer auto loans generated through the dealership while they are pulling out of floorplan relationships. In extreme cases, more common recently, if banks do not have *both* the mortgage and the floorplan notes, they stop buying retail paper. This makes it next to impossible to sell cars. The dealer needs to keep selling and reordering the right

cars to both make enough gross profit income to pay his employees
and mortgage payments and to keep his monthly floorplan interest
expense in line.

Once Citizens, or some other floorplan lender sends a letter
terminating the floorplan relationship, the dealer is forced into a high-
risk, high-interest pool, where he can easily choke on the exorbitant
floorplan interest expenses. If there are no other players to take over
the floorplan financing, the dealership is doomed.

The most recent and media-overlooked case of this was with
GMAC, General Motors finance arm. GMAC essentially got out of
the retail loan business and began pulling out of the GM dealer floorplan business during the second half of 2008. They received $5 billion
in government TARP funds (Troubled Assets Relief Fund) from the
Bush administration. There was nothing in the TARP fund documents compelling GMAC to provide either dealer floorplan financing,
or customer loans. So they took the money and virtually ceased all
business activity. Nice.

Why Do Banks Provide Floorplan Financing?

Banks engage in floorplan lending in order to earn interest profits.
The interest rates vary by either the U.S. prime rate or the London
Interbank Rate (LIBOR). LIBOR is based on the interest rates banks
charge each other when loaning one another money. As an example,
a three million dollar floorplan line to cover 150 new cars at a rate
of 7% APR costs the dealership roughly $210,000 per year in inter-
est. Often, there are other daily (per diem) fees associated with each
vehicle as well as insurance costs driving this expense even higher.
Floorplan is paid monthly, directly from the dealer's business account
to his floorplan lender.

Manufacturers are extremely eager to get the new inventory off
their books and paid for as quickly as they are built. Franchise contracts insist on a dealer-bank agreement, which allows the factory to

draw payment from the dealer's floorplan account simultaneous to a vehicle's production. All is billed and transferred electronically. Often, manufacturers draft against dealer floorplan lines even before vehicles are loaded up and in transit to dealership lots! In fact, provisions in franchise contracts preempt dealers from even challenging this practice unless the undelivered vehicle(s) in question are ten days late. Of course, policing this policy is next to impossible for the dealer. He would be tripping over dollars to pick up nickels by paying an office person to audit every factory delivery.

However, even if the average time to receive a vehicle were five days, banks are still collecting some additional $20,000 per year in interest on vehicles that are still in factory transit. Essentially, the factories' sales job is done once a dealer pays for the car. Special rebate and low finance rate incentive blessings only come when dealers are not reordering. Remember, as a rule, factories are unconcerned with dealer margins, only that they continue to take cars. Chrysler has been known to prepay six months of dealers' floorplan interest charges up front, directly to its dealers, so they'd take cars. Of course, the dealer's death comes by a thousand paper cuts if he doesn't move them within those six months.

Banking in Dealer World is a necessary evil. Lenders are all too ready to loan money in the good times—exploiting the industry in any and every imaginable way. Just like with every American consumer, banks make money on dealership mortgages, dealer floorplan, working-capital loans, and consumer auto loans. They even make money on every swipe of a consumer's credit card at the service lane or parts department—getting it from both ends—consumers and the dealership.

When things turn down however, these institutions ditch their dealers. Finding and maintaining floorplan sources is a constant challenge and worry for today's dealer. And despite the sales slowdown and need for less inventory on dealership lots, curtailment of floorplan limits are a major reason why you see fewer and fewer vehicles in stock to choose from.

GMAC, after receiving $5 billion in (Troubled Asset Relief Funds) TARP bailout money—which you, as the taxpayer, funded—curbed its floorplan relationships with many dealers. It terminated some loan contracts and shortened those remaining to a period of ninety days. At each ninety-day juncture, GMAC reviews the account and either terminates or extends the relationship. The renewals require approximately $17,000 in dealer-funded administrative and processing fees in order to freshen-up the paperwork.

This is yet another example of why government bailouts of the financial institutions (with your money) hasn't helped you. You pay for the lender's mistakes in order to have fewer places to shop for a better price and fewer cars to look at when you get there. Rear-ended, run over, and crushed—with your own wallet! How did it all start? Read on.

Sixteen

How We Stopped Selling Seven Million Cars a Year

. . . and What It Cost You

*"Failure is the opportunity to begin
again, more intelligently."*

—HENRY FORD
Founder of Ford Motor Co. & Innovator of
Assembly-Line Manufacturing (1863–1947)

et's revisit Jack and Jill Hill for a moment. Jack and Jill have a mortgage on their home. Who collects interest on that debt? Jack has high credit card balances and in the past had trouble making more than the minimum payments. Who enjoys the profits of that interest income? Jill, the pragmatist, has changed them both over to debit cards now, ensuring their debt doesn't grow. Who gets the $1.50 for every swipe? Banks. They are involved in nearly every transaction of our lives.

Since mortgage foreclosure inventory has become the topic du jour—as the dastardly culprit behind the collapse of our financial system—nobody has taken the cue to look at how banks finance automobiles. Look at the trouble they're in with *appreciating* assets like homes and commercial real estate. How much worse, then, is the mess they can make with *depreciating* assets such as cars?

The FDIC (Federal Deposit Insurance Corporation) and SEC (Securities and Exchange Commission) both regulate the valuation of assets on a bank's balance sheet: the FDIC in the areas of insuring depositors against bank failure and the SEC in the areas of banks' ability to buy and sell securities. The mechanism the SEC uses to control the banks is a regulation known as the mark-to-market rule of accounting.

Government Accounting Rules and How They Crush The Economy

In a recent *Forbes* magazine article Newt Gingrich quotes Chief Economist Brian S. Wesbury and Bob Stein of First Trust Portfolios of Chicago; *"It is true that the root of this crisis is bad mortgage loans, but probably 70% of the real crisis that we face today is caused by mark-to-market accounting in an illiquid market. What's most fascinating is the Treasury is selling its plan as a way to put a bottom in mortgage pool price, tipping its hat to the problem of mark-to-market accounting without acknowledging it. It is a real shame there is so little discussion of this reality."*[18]

Speaker Gingrich goes on to add, *"If regulators on their own—or Congress, if regulators fail to use their discretion—can fix 70% of the financial crisis by changing the mark-to-market accounting rule, we should change the rule first before attempting to pass another reevaluated bailout package."*[19]

While writing this book, I spoke with many businesspeople in all walks of life. Some had heard of mark-to-market (or at least claimed to), a few had never heard of it (or at least were honest enough to admit it), and, *none* had any idea how the rule impacts the economy.

The rule says that the value of a financial instrument is based upon the current market price for that financial instrument. Great, but what's a financial instrument, you say? A financial instrument is an asset that a person or entity can use as *collateral* to buy stocks, bonds and borrow cash. It only makes logical sense to assume if you want to buy $100 worth of stock on credit and use an asset as collateral to do so; that asset must be worth (at least) $100, right? It only makes sense that if the stock value dives to a value of $0 later on, the buyer has enough cashable assets to pay for the loss.

However, the dangers of this rule in tough economic times is sorely underestimated. In fact, mark-to-market ignites a spiral of self-fulfilling destruction to our economy. Why? Mark-to-market also says; as average home prices drop, banks must reduce the value of all the homes they've mortgaged down to those amounts. This is irrespective of whether the particular bank's homeowners are faithful in paying their mortgage payments or not. As those average values drop, so goes the value of the bank, according to the rule. The less a bank, or in this case—*all* the banks are worth on their balance sheets—the less they can loan out to new borrowers.

Here's an example. Meet the fictitious Bank of Boomtown. Boomtown has loaned money against 100 homes, all mortgaged for $250,000 apiece. They did so, at a time when each of the homes would easily resell for $400,000 or more. On these deals, Boomtown is ahead of the game with $15 million in equity:

TABLE 17:   **Mark to Market Rule of Accounting Impact on Bank Equity**

$400,000	Value of Average Home
$250,000	Mortgage of Average Home
$150,000	Equity of Average Home
100	Number of Homes in Bank Portfolio
$15,000,000	**Bank Equity**

Banks lend up to ten times their equity. Therefore, this $15 million equity position rapidly turns into $150 million in new additional loans the bank makes available to consumers. Obviously, this kind of monetary availability fuels economic growth.

More Loans = More Home Sales = Less Supply = Higher Prices = Higher Mark-to-Market Values = More Equity in the Banks = More Loans . . . And the circle of success repeats feeding the economy with growth and vitality.

Now, consider today's situation where Countrywide Financial (mortgage company) spits out foreclosure sales—countrywide. Both Freddie Mac and Fannie Mae are on their collective fanny; puking out more foreclosure sales. And the excess supply of houses on the market sends home prices plummeting. Instead of those mortgaged homes being valued at $400,000 or more, they are worth only $200,000 apiece. Boomtown's customers may be paying their mortgages just fine and on time, mind you. Nonetheless, here is what mark-to-market does to Boomtown's equity:

TABLE 18:   **Mark to Market Impact following Housing Value Crash**

$200,000	Mark-to-Market value of Average Home
$250,000	Mortgage of Average Home
($50,000)	Equity of Average Home
100	Number of Homes in Bank Portfolio
($5,000,000)	**Bank Equity After Crash**

After adjusting to the market, the bank's $15 million equity—which they had parlayed into an additional $150 million in loans—suddenly turns into a quick $50 million dollar loss (on paper). This causes them to chase, call, or sell every loan they have in order to make up for a now $200 million dollar reduction in lending ability.

The cycle reverses: Less Loans = Less Home Sales = More Supply = Lower Prices = Lower Mark-to-Market Values = Less Equity in the Banks = Less Loans . . . And the cycle spirals downward feeding itself into an economic depression.

Because Boomtown is measured not by the cash flow their mortgage portfolio is generating in profits each month, but rather by the industry as a whole, they can no longer make loans. The restriction on

Boomtown's lending is based upon a pure and simple accounting rule, not reality. Now take every home mortgage bank in the nation and put them in the same pickle-barrel. What have you got? You have a situation where trillions of dollars are now unavailable to consumers. Less folks can borrow money to buy a house, so prices erode. This perpetuates the cycle of lower and lower home values.

Those trillions of dollars now out of the lending supply, much of which could be added back into the economy—literally with the stroke of a pen—has instead been remedied with $700 billion in taxpayer TARP funds. The problem: as long as the rule is in effect in its current form, those assets will continue to be troubled, until banks have enough equity to begin lending again.

Of course, banks will not have enough equity to begin lending again until the assets become worth more—a maddening cycle. Throwing billions of dollars at the problem is like pouring a hot cup of coffee into Boston Harbor and expecting to see it in Tokyo Bay. Some economists say the federal government will have to purchase and remove these mortgage portfolios from the banks' balance sheets altogether in order to spur lending and reverse the spiral. This will require nationalization of the banks—government common stock ownership—similar to what has occurred with GM and Chrysler.

How does this affect the automotive industry? Mark-to-market and the chokehold it has created on banking as we know it feeds violently on the automotive finance markets—both in the form of new auto loan approvals and floorplan credit lines. In the case of Boomtown Bank, since they must call so many loans, a dealer's $3 million floorplan line is a great place to start. Jumping out of the auto loan business is also an effective way of reducing bank exposure.

Home Foreclosures = Bank Tightening = Job Losses & Less Auto Loans

Financing upside-down customers is becoming more and more difficult: a major reason why we are selling fewer automobiles today.

Since the average consumer is $4,700 upside-down and the banks have to start somewhere—reining-in excess loans outstanding—the automotive market is depressed. Do you see the connection? Good. You are way ahead of the federal government. Either the government is missing this point or it is intentionally overlooking the issue. Why? Perhaps it relishes the idea of nationalizing the banks that support the auto industry rather than just the industry itself.

The government has attempted—anemically as it may appear—to rectify, at least, the floorplan issue. This would benefit you by sustaining more dealerships in the marketplace, allowing greater price competition, and increasing product selection for you to shop. It's new program (and associated acronym) is called: TALF (Term Asset-backed securities Loan Facility). Like most fancy names and acronyms, danger looms in the details behind the catch-phrase. In my personal experience, *more* than two capital letters next to each other spells trouble. The following was taken from The NADA website. My remarks are in parenthesis.

"Dealers rely on floorplan financing to buy vehicles from the manufacturers. The average floorplan loan for a dealer is $ 4.9 million, and dealers collectively hold approximately $100 billion in floorplan inventory. These floorplan loans are obtained from a variety of sources: captive finance companies, national banks, regional banks, credit unions, etc.

In order to extend this credit, the floorplan lenders need capital, and they obtain it from a variety of sources. One key source of capital for the floorplan lenders is the floorplan securitization market (similar to the housing mortgage market). To access capital through this market, floorplan lenders bundle dealer floorplan loans together into what are called asset-backed securities (ABS) and then sell these ABSs to institutional investors (to restore their cash reserves and start the lending cycle all over again).

(Prior to the 4th quarter of 2008), the floorplan securitization market was operating quite well, providing very
efficiently priced capital for floorplan lenders. Floorplan
securitizations were good investments and attracted a lot of
buyers. In fact, floorplan securitizations were generally rated
AAA. Three examples of dealer funding supported by ABS:
SBA guaranteed loans for dealership operations.
Retail Auto Financing.
Dealer floorplan loans.

Why am I alarmed at the good news? Every automobile sold to
every dealership is over-billed by as much as 2%–3% of the vehicle's
MSRP. Banks over-fund this amount to the automakers at the time
the vehicle is shipped to dealers. The car companies use this money,
interest-free, for up to three months, before returning it to their dealers in cash.

The whole scheme was initially set up, allegedly, for dealer cash
flow benefits. Today however, it is clearly a free cash float for automakers. Additionally, automakers assess up to $600 per vehicle on roughly
80% of their vehicle shipments. They list these charges as special
dealer marketing fees. These two bank-funded items, which appear on
virtually every car and truck sold in America today, total no less than
$1,500 per vehicle on average.

So is the program really asset based or more smoke and mirrors
that got us into the same type of trouble we have with housing? Would
you loan somebody $21,500 backed by only $20,000 worth of collateral? Maybe. As long as you knew the loan wasn't *truly* asset based. In
this case, $1,500 of every vehicle on the floorplan market—$100 billion worth according to NADA—is *non*-asset based. Yet the program
acronym indicates otherwise.

My point is this: what gives the government such expertise to
require banks to value even quality home mortgage portfolios as toxic,
while promoting floorplan lending as asset based? They don't know

what they are doing. Somebody comes up with an idea that sounds good at the time and bingo! Ready, Fire, Aim.

I am happy for the dealers and consumers in the short-term. However, successive short-term thinking has gotten us where we are today—in trouble. According to NADA (my comments in parenthesis once more), *"Without adequate floorplan financing, even a well-capitalized dealer will cease operations in a matter of a few weeks. (The TALF) will also provide greater access to retail credit because many floorplan lenders also are major providers of retail automotive credit. Normalization of floorplan lending will empower dealers to place orders from the manufacturers. In sum, the Federal Reserve's action is exactly what the nation's ailing economy needs at every level."*

Pulling The Band-Aid Off Slowly Intensifies the Pain

NADA's statement is mostly true, except for the last sentence. If and when mark-to-market accounting kicks in, the whole house of cards folds up. What happens when banks liquidate the inventories of thousands of failed and terminated dealers nationwide? Will even the healthy floorplan portfolios be devalued as mark-to-market dictates? How about the average consumer auto loan remaining $4,700 upside-down and the repossession losses resulting from unemployment? Will they affect healthy lenders auto credit portfolios? Mark-to-market does not discriminate. One bank's losses become another's asset valuation, equity valuation, and ability to loan money. Money supply drives the whole market, in every sector.

Upwards of a trillion dollars is on the line in a jump-ball of floorplan and consumer auto loans. All of this is potentially removed from the credit market if the auto industry tips the way of home values—all at the hands of mark-to-market and TALF. $1 trillion in potential credit will be removed from the credit markets. Disastrous. Catastrophic. Macro economists, specialists in a subject on which I proclaim to be no expert, could probably quantify the financial cataclysm that would ensue:

No Auto Loans = No Sales = No Manufacturing = No Wages = No Sales

TALF will work, provided that mark-to-market is addressed in a big way, shifting it to a performance-based financial model. Banks writing good loans should be rewarded instead of being thrown into the same pickle-barrel as those acting irresponsibly. Not dissimilar to the Rule of 78s, mark-to-market functional practicality has gone out the window along with the telegraph and rotary-dial phone. Our government has not seen the light on this one—or it doesn't want to.

Seventeen

How You Funded the Union's Purchase of GM and Chrysler
... and Why Your Wallet Is Still Open

"A government big enough to give you everything you want, is strong enough to take everything you have."

—THOMAS JEFFERSON
Third U.S. President & Author of the
Declaration of Independence (1743–1826)

Prior to the end of his second term, George W. Bush approved $25 billion in federal loans to General Motors, GMAC, Chrysler LLC and Chrysler Credit Corp. The money was given up-front on December 29, 2008, with conditions set forth for the companies to receive additional disbursements following transfer of power to the Obama Administration in 2009. Bush's conditions specified the creation of a viable turnaround plan by the automakers, as well as wage and contract concessions by the UAW. The UAW never made those concessions before the next round of government disbursements was to be approved. In fact, they didn't even sit down to talk with GM and Chrysler until two days before Congress was to review the automakers' progress.

Most of the industry players were elated at the time of Bush's initial loan approval. Vendors and suppliers got paid. Dealers remained open for business, despite the dark economic climate. And the assembly lines kept rolling. In retrospect however, Bush threw taxpayer funds out the window in an effort to save companies that ultimately went bankrupt anyway. Arguably, more important than even the billions in squandered cash, Bush opened the door to the nationalization of select American businesses *and* confiscation of the personal property and legal rights of others.

The Laws of Investor Protection and Why They Are Critical to You

The federal bankruptcy code clearly outlines the level of protection or risk for investors and stakeholders in any corporation. Bondholders come first. Meaning, even if a company must be liquidated into cash in order to refund bondholder investments, bondholders are entitled to *all* their money back (or as much as can be recovered through the liquidation). This occurs, according to the law, regardless if there is any money leftover for anyone else in the game. Bondholders rule the roost in this regard.

This bankruptcy rule is designed to encourage everyone—from little old ladies to you and me—to invest our retirement funds (and cash we've earned, inherited or saved) into corporate bonds. Bond purchasers must have confidence they will get their money back, even if things go badly for the companies they have invested in. This takes pressure and risk off of the banking system so banks can loan companies all the money they need, thus providing the private sector with a means of relatively low-risk investments that yield decent returns.

Bonds are sold as either short-term or long-term investments. Meaning, investors agree to have their money tied-up for a predetermined period of time and receive their return in an agreed lump-sum at the end of that term. Think of it like a bank certificate of deposit (CD) on steroids. Except bonds, unlike CDs, can be sold and traded on the market through brokers. And nobody gives you a toaster or alarm clock for buying a bond, like banks selling CDs sometimes do.

Preferred shareholders are next in the line of priorities, according to the bankruptcy courts. They are essentially "tweeners"; falling somewhere in between a bondholder (protection-wise) and a common shareholder (return-wise). This class of investor owns stock in the company, but has no voting rights. These stakeholders count on guaranteed dividends and stock value increases as their means of gaining a return on their investment.

Just like with bondholders, the amount of preferred shares in investor hands is viewed as debt the company owes, according to the government. When "loaning" bailout TARP money to banks and other companies, the government does so by purchasing preferred stock. This saddles the entities with debt, making it more difficult for them to borrow money from banks. When looking to nationalize a company, the government trades its preferred shares for common stock. This gives the government managerial voting rights and board seats, while instantaneously relieving debt from the company's balance sheet. Common stock is not viewed as corporate debt like bonds and preferred shares are.

Common shareholders retain the least amount of investor protections and commonly get wiped out in bankruptcy, dependent upon which type of bankruptcy is approved by the courts. In the case of total liquidation, they may receive some money back, but not until each superior class of investors (bondholders first and preferred shareholders second) get *all of their* money back 100%.

Common shareholders assume the most amount of investment risk, but retain all of the managerial voting rights. It is the common shareholders who run the company. They can receive dividends if approved by the board of directors (which they control), so long as preferred shareholders are paid their dividends first. Mostly however, common shareholders count on growth of stock value in the marketplace allowing them to sell their shares for more than they purchased them for. Some folks make a living out of buying and selling common

stocks, hawking over their computers all day long—buying and selling—in a practice known as day trading.

Unions and other vendor or contract interests come dead last in
bankruptcy law. Meaning, promises to investors legally outrank everyone else who may be owed money, contractually or not. But this is
not how the bankruptcies of GM and Chrysler were handled. Other
interests were placed ahead of the investors: a dangerous, politically
motivated precedent that will forever change the way you should view
your legal rights.

The companies were not liquidated for the bondholders benefit, they were restructured for the UAW's benefit. The bondholders
were refunded as little as 29¢ on the dollar. And the UAW now owns
the automakers. Not the kettle of fish anyone signed-up for—except
perhaps the union—which remains the beneficiary of this unconstitutional carnage. Here's how their plan came together.

A New (and Dangerous) Class of Corporate Stakeholder
That Trumps Everybody Else

President Bush's order was a godsend to the UAW. You'd think the
organization would have been happy with his decision to keep shifts
running and union members paid. Well, they were, in a backhanded
sort of way. As evidenced by the rhetoric of UAW President Ron
Gettelfinger, the union relished avoiding *traditional* bankruptcy, where
their contracts would have been shredded in court. Instead, Bush's
taxpayer gift provided just enough breathing room to operate the companies until the Obama administration came into power, a President
who would not have won his office without union support. The following excerpts are taken, with thanks, from the UAW website.[20]

DETROIT–"We're pleased that the Bush administration
has acted today to provide urgently needed emergency bridge
loans to America's auto companies and to pursue a process for

restructuring outside of bankruptcy ... We will work with the Obama administration and the new Congress to ensure that these unfair conditions are removed, as we join in the coming months with all stakeholders to create a viable future for the U.S. auto industry."

The Obama administration had bigger ideas for its constituency than simply overturning some of Bush's stipulations requiring union concessions. UAW failure to sit down with either GM or Chrysler to even discuss the matter, virtually guaranteed the automakers would not receive further federal assistance. Lack of additional government cash assured the companies' demise into bankruptcy. Except under the Obama administration and its automotive industry task force—led by Car Czar Steven Rattner—bankruptcy would look far different for the UAW. In an Obama-structured bankruptcy, all the stakeholder protections would be inverted. The UAW would own the companies.

The government fired General Motors' CEO Rick Wagoner and more eloquently terminated Bob Nardelli of Chrysler, as it prepared to get rough with corporate bondholders. At one point, President Obama called the *greedy* class of investors "Un-American," for rebuking the administration's offer of 29¢ on the dollar.

And under task force recommendation, the government closed 789 dealers' businesses (profitable or not) and are declining to renew 1,124 dealer contracts in October 2010. In the meantime, those dealers can no longer order new vehicles or parts. Folks who have personally guaranteed their mortgages and floorplan lines were forced to go bankrupt at the hands of a politically motivated totalitarian scheme.

Emerging from the melee; the UAW, the U.S. federal government, and even the Canadian government now own these automakers. Our government just bought it for them in a rigged deal that restructured two global corporations faster than you or I could clear a fruit stand through bankruptcy court. The reported legal expenses totaled $80 million dollars for GM alone. And your tax dollars, along with bondholder investments derived from regular folks' 401k retirement funds were used to pay for it all.

The whole deal was placed in the union's lap by our government. Why? Using your money to fund a UAW constituency provides politicians with massive campaign contributions and a block of votes one million strong in return.

How UAW Contracts Ran Over Their Employers and Crushed Your Wallet

The UAW's historic apathy towards the competitive condition of its employers is dizzying. On September 24, 2007 at approximately 11:00 am. EDT, the roughly 73,000 General Motors workers represented by the United Auto Workers union went on strike against the company.[21] The first nationwide strike against GM since 1970 was expected to idle 59 plants and facilities for an indefinite period of time. Talks broke down after more than 20 straight days of bargaining failed to produce a new contract. Major issues proving to be stumbling blocks for an agreement included wages, benefits, job security, and investments in U.S. facilities.[22] Just one year later, GM executives appealed to the federal government for financial assistance.

The most significant UAW contract clause—known as Jobs Banks—forced GM, Chrysler, and Ford to perpetually pay the wages and benefits of some 500,000 union workers, regardless of business climate or production needs. This is to say, while the industry shrank from 16.5 million units to 9.5 million units, these companies could do nothing to bring their production schedules in line with the decline in business.

Created in 1984, jobs banks were really designed to keep UAW workers on the payroll, even if they weren't working on the assembly line. The UAW's 2007 contract with General Motors states these idle workers still receive 100% of their pay, if they simply report to a jobs bank each week. Furthermore, even if they don't report—even if they sit at home and watch *Geraldo*—they still receive 85% of their pay for two-and-a-half years. The program really means unemployed workers continue to be paid full wages by their employer no matter what.[23]

The union and even the manufacturers have defended jobs banks, by claiming the skills required to build automobiles necessitate workers to be *ready* in the wings, able to jump back onto assembly lines whenever needed. Presuming they are correct, this theoretically occurs when more cars need to be built. Well, when is that going to happen? When domestic market share and/or the U.S. auto market increases substantially? Is that day imminently approaching? Truthfully, it is not coming any time soon.

Meanwhile Toyota, Honda, Nissan, Hyundai, Kia and BMW—along with their investors—have U.S. plants in areas of the country where workers do not receive such entitlements. In their world, when a shift needs to be shut down, it is shut down. Period. These manufacturers do not build an excessive quantity of cars, only to destroy their customer's equity—and corporate profits—with huge rebates and rental company deals *before* they even leave the plant. But this was the practice of both Chrysler and GM (and Ford until it negotiated itself out of the jobs banks clause on February 10, 2009 by threatening the UAW with the consequences of a traditional bankruptcy). Freedom from government TARP control would mean Ford could right-size itself through layoffs, a luxury not afforded to GM and Chrysler once they accepted the goverment funds. They simply could not lay people off and downsize on their own. The UAW Jobs Banks clause said so.

The more rental car deals and rebates an automaker plays with in dealing with overproduction issues, the faster their vehicles depreciate in the marketplace. This means that the overproduction dictated by the union's contract depreciated vehicles—like yours—even faster. This is but one area where the union affects consumers—like you—directly. The excess negative equity keeps you in debt and prevents you from trading your car more often. Moreover, the expense of these incentives devastated those companies financially.

Here is my favorite parable from one of my kids' favorite books, Shel Silverstein's classic, *The Giving Tree*.[24] I trust you will clearly see the parallels:

It is a little story of few words about a beautiful tree that loves a little boy. She is his leafy playground, his provider of shade and comfort, and his apple bearer. Giving to him and loving him makes the tree happy. But the little boy takes and takes from the tree. He disappears for long stretches during his life, returning only when he needs something from the tree. He asks for money and she gives him her apples to sell. He asks for a house so she offers her branches for the lumber to build one. The boy, as a man, asks for a boat and the giving tree sacrifices her trunk in order to build one.

The once majestic tree, now dissected down to a stump tethered by roots, is all that remains. The boy has taken everything she had. Still, when he returns once more as an old man, she offers him all she has left to rest upon.

How Unions Will Gain Greater Control of the Price You Pay in the Future

Interestingly enough, legislation called "The Employee Freedom of Choice Act," nicknamed "Card Check," aims to expand the union presence in our economy by 2010. If passed, it will change operations at car dealerships across America as well as at automakers such as Toyota, Honda, BMW, and others. In fact, any automobile company manufacturing in the United States will be subject to the same demise as GM and Chrysler. Jobs banks stipulations may necessitate rebates and rental car company sales by all automakers. Consumers like you will be rear-ended and run over with higher prices and more depreciation.

Doing the same thing over and over again, while expecting a different result, is the definition of insanity. Card Check, along with the unconstitutional intervention of government bureaucracy in employment contract negotiations, will result in more vehicle over-production, more consumer vehicle depreciation, and more misery for the auto industry and its consumers. President Obama has committed to signing Card Check into law.

Same S#!T, Different Day: How the "New" GM & Chrysler are Back to Their Old Tricks Again (Already)

After clearing the decks of all debt and obligations, the rescued automakers are back at it again; making the same mistakes, chasing the same red herrings. It didn't take them long. The whole premise of turning around their businesses by firing dealers is simply preposterous. Obama's automotive industry task force took a look at the sell-through numbers of foreign franchises such as, Lexus and Toyota, and decided to model the domestics' dealer network numbers accordingly. According to testimony before the House Committee on Energy and Commerce, the automakers were instructed by the task force to right-size their dealer networks in preparation for government takeover.

GM and Chrysler executives—never to waste an opportunity for political retribution—took advantage of the opportunity to enact their decades-old run at dealer genocide. This time, with no price-tag attached, this type of initiative proved far too expensive to complete while formerly under the restrictions of state laws.

The real play was for the automakers to get rid of dealers offering competing brands in shared facilities (also known as duals in industry jargon) or to grab the franchise from one operator and give it to another favored candidate already representing a sister brand. All this, without having to pay for it. Terminating some dealers viewed as less than historically cooperative with the factory was frosting on the cake for them. The hangings were carried out irrespective of some dealers recently constructing new facilities (with mortgages they personally signed to do so).

I lived this nightmare through GM's Project 2000 Initiative. All General Motors dealers were instructed to watch a special broadcast in May 1997 by Ron Zarella, GM's new Marketing Chief. GM, at the time, required all their dealers to install and maintain special satellite dishes for such broadcasts. Previously at Bausch and Lomb, Zarella was a true outsider to our industry. GM brought him in to solve the myriad problems with its receding market share and sagging stock market value. Replay after replay, we were hit with the driest, most horrifying message ever imaginable to the GM dealer network: the GM Channel Plan.

The GM Channel Plan called for the reduction of the number of GM dealers by offering more GM brands per location. This meant combining all Pontiac, Buick, and GMC dealers into one dealership location in each market. Chevrolet, Oldsmobile, and Cadillac were also to be combined into separate dealerships. In the most rural markets, they planned to combine all GM brands into a single dealership location. Their order of priority was; channel, location, dealer—in that order. Every GM brand and every GM dealership location felt the financial tremble on the Richter Scale—all except for Saturn—Roger Smith's commitment of $6 billion in GM investments was not to be touched!

Pontiac, Buick, GMC in one dealership location = On Channel
Chevrolet, Oldsmobile, Cadillac in one dealership location = On Channel
All Brands together in one dealership location (rural markets) = On Channel
Ragsdale Pontiac-Cadillac = Target On Your Back

I had just purchased the majority interest in my first dealership. I had set a personal goal to become a dealer before age 30, and was blessed with the opportunity to do so. I was employed as the dealership's general manager for five years prior, and it felt good to have a place of my own. The store had not made a lot of money, but it was fun to run and sold a lot of cars—at least in a "cream of the *crap*" kind of definition.

We had grown the dealership to become the largest Pontiac retailer in Massachusetts and the second largest in New England. The scores of our sales and service customer satisfaction surveys were the highest from Albany, NY to Bangor, ME. We had amassed 350 leases in our portfolio; customers who were teed up to deliver another 150 sales every year via lease renewals alone. But Mr. Zarella just announced that Pontiac and Cadillac didn't go together anymore. So my life was about to change.

Following the broadcast, the car auctions were noisy with every rumor possible. After all, no matter how well my dealership was doing for the automaker, someone in a room somewhere decided I was unnecessary. And that was that. Immediately following the fanfare across *Automotive News*, a GM team went forth and overpaid the first 20 willing dealers ridiculous sums of money to sell out. They overpaid for the easy ones. The rest of us *Misfits in Toyland* received a visit from one of the team members. Their offers were low and the rumors they spread about the marketplace vicious.

I have always found employees supremely focused on buyout or sellout rumors. I would learn to chalk such behavior up to basic human self-preservation. To a larger point, GM's rumor mongering was designed to weaken dealers financially in order to aid in purchase negotiations. I hope they've "saved" a lot of money with this practice, because it destroys dealership employee focus on consumers. Lack of focus costs customers every time. Workers cannot satisfy customers while they are worried about their own job security. My dad has always taught me "you cannot *save* your way into a profit." GM was tripping over dollars to pick up nickels though.

Déjà Vu

Not long after they concluded their boardroom-driven shattering of many lives, GM shut down and bought out every Oldsmobile dealer in the country, modifying their Channel Plan *yet again*. The local Oldsmobile dealer who had attempted to get my Cadillac franchise under the Channel Plan closed his dealership. Ron Zarella resigned from GM in an embarrassing scandal of personal misrepresentation and resume-fraud. Mr. Zarella went back to selling contact lenses at Bausch and Lomb, and I went back to running my store.

I bring your attention to GM's Channel Plan failure because we are seeing it all over again. If history is any lesson, the initiative proved nothing more than a former contact lens guy's *failed* idea of turning around General Motors.

Steven Rattner, who resigned as head of President Obama's automotive task force, did so less than thirty days after executing his dealer-shuttering program. Another industry outsider coming in, blowing up family businesses, and then riding out of town after spending your tax dollars like a drunken cowboy. People like these are the *Smartest Guys in the Room* for their fifteen minutes of fame. Afterward, they leave the rest of us to pick up the pieces. Why should they care? What skin do they have left in the game? They're onto something else before the ink is dry on the deal. The rest of us remember that doing the same thing over and over again—expecting a different result—is the definition of insanity. Let's do the math.

Thousands of dealer employers have either lost their ability to pay mortgages on empty facilities or "punted" by attempting to run *used-only* car lots in violation of town ordinances. They have had to cope with the loss of their banking relationships in a capital-intensive business. Most have been forced to pack it in by closing their dealerships or going bankrupt. Those forced down these routes have laid-off an average of 53 employees per location. The aggregate government dice-roll on dealership workers forced out of a job—due to the Rattner/Obama strategy—hovers around 100,000 and growing. Quite an accomplishment for now-resigned Car Czar Steven Rattner and the President who averted Congressional oversight by appointing him.

The elderly have lost retirement investments along with their faith in federal corporate bankruptcy laws. The same laws that were enacted to protect their investments were trounced for political reasons in order to ingratiate a stronger, more liberal constituency. I dare say Tom Brokaw's *Greatest Generation* is now referred to by our president as *Un-American*.

And you, the taxpayer have fewer dealerships to shop for price, fewer to shop for selection, and fewer locations to service your automobiles. You have dealership bankruptcies and property foreclosures in your community, along with increased local unemployment due to laid-off dealership workers. You own the contingent liability of Chrysler and GM to fund through your tax dollars regardless of what you drive. Rear-ended, run over and crushed.

Is your industry, business, or job next on the federal government's hit list? Are you *too big to fail*, like the banks, automakers, and AIG, or *too small to care about*, like the dealers and their employees whose demise you funded through your votes and tax dollars?

Eighteen

Green Technology, Fuel Price Manipulation, Selective Stimulus

... Great Ideas Your Children Will Pay For

"Government's view of the economy could be summed up in a few short phrases: If it moves, tax it. If it keeps moving, regulate it. And if it stops moving, subsidize it."

—RONALD REAGAN
Thirty-Ninth U.S. President (1911–2004)

Alas, the road to hell is paved with good intentions. Not exclusively, of course. Bad intentions also get us there quickly. However, in the case of Corporate Average Fuel Economy (CAFE) standards, carbon emissions controls, and legislating mandatory technological advances, the Obama administration is building a HOV lane to Hades. This multi-passenger-only, 100 M.P.G., zero-emissions dreamboat ride is terrible for the auto industry and even worse for your wallet!

Green At Any Cost

In the same way the government can be an enabler to some players' selfish interests in exchange for its own—such as unions and banks—it demonstrates an equal ability to impede automakers and the entire U.S. automobile industry overall, in order to get what it wants. President Obama's EPA-driven increase in CAFE standards by executive order—while well intentioned—will cripple the industry. Increasing fuel economy in the auto industry addresses 27% of all the petroleum consumption occurring in the U.S. Consequently, it is a valid concern. However, therein lies a bit of a red herring and atrocious timing.

First, the red herring: Ten years ago, we would scrap 8 old junkers for every 10 new ones we put on the road. The impact of increased fuel economy technology back then was close to a 1:1 ratio.[25] Meaning, advances in the replacement market had an almost immediate impact.

This ratio dipped to 0.6:1 in 2005. Meaning, we'd only junk 6 old clunkers out of every 10 we put on the road. Those successive declines in cars coming off the road, along with the constant growth in new vehicle sales, has grown the number of cars in operation by 50 million units in the last ten years. The growth of units in U.S. operation has occurred at percentage gains similar to our population increases. In an effort to address this, Congress spent $3 billion in stimulus money to shred more junkers. $3 billion to take between 666,666.67 and 857,142.86 clunkers off the road, depending upon what folks qualified for. But these are the least and most units they could have mathematically bought off the road with all that money.

What is missing from CAFE supporters' calculations is the limited short-term effect the standards will truly have. Today, there are some 248 million vehicles on U.S. roads. The net effect of new vehicle registrations versus clunker scrappage will require almost 25 years to replace the U.S. fleet with more efficient models. In that time, technology will move in the direction it is heading anyway—away from the internal combustion motor. This brings me to my next point—atrocious timing.

Which horse should automakers ride? Fiscal responsibility, consumer choice, technology, or government mandates? You see, the government believes it is pushing technology through CAFE, but it is really rear-ending you here. Have you noticed how *well* the car companies have managed their businesses in the past? Does the government think these folks can really walk and chew gum at the same time?

While attempting to comply with the new standards in an affordable way, automakers' eyes will be off the ball in developing true alternative technologies. If the goal is to dump the internal combustion engine in exchange for batteries, hydrogen, and natural gas, why then would the government focus automakers' attention on finding new combustion management ideas? It's time to prioritize the economic realities of the business—and our country—by realizing the immediate goals of economic improvement *before* ecological wish-lists. Sadly, ecology must come second until people have jobs again. I'm sorry everyone can't have their cake and eat it too. But that is the truth.

Even those who argue that automakers can and must develop efficiency in fuel economy and carbon emissions at a greater rate cannot deny its cost to consumers. Compliance with the new regulation will cost you another $3,000 or more in transmission upgrades and engine cylinder shut-down mechanisms, according to Gloria Berquist, vice president of the Auto Alliance.[26]

Other analysts claim this technology is already available, so getting it into place won't be a problem. The added components, in their opinion, would *only* cost consumers $1,000 more on every new car. Either figure is too much right now.

Consumers are already battling an average $4,700 upside-down situation in an illiquid loan market. Any more burden and the consumer snaps, but not before being dumped by the banks as nonviable credit candidates. Meaning, auto loans are tough enough to get now, never mind tossing on another $1,000 to $3,000. Can the cost increases be absorbed by already insolvent automakers? Obviously not. Not while selling some 7 million fewer units annually than they did just two years ago.

The industry is already attempting to prioritize hybrid technology and sales in the marketplace. Unfortunately, the price difference between a standard combustion model and its hybrid counterpart is untenable for most consumers. For example, the 2008 Honda Civic Sedan starts at $15,505. Its hybrid cousin starts at $23,650—an $8,000 price differential. The hybrid gets 11 miles per gallon more on the highway than the standard model. For a cash buyer paying $8,000 more for the hybrid and driving an average of 15,000 miles per year, here is the payback in years:

TABLE 19: **Years of Driving Required in Order to Financially Justify Your Hybrid**

Price Per Gallon	Gallons @ 34 MPG	Gallons @ 45 MPG	Annual Dollar Savings	Payback in Years
$2.00	441	333	$216	37
$2.50	441	333	$270	30
$3.00	441	333	$324	25
$3.50	441	333	$377	21
$4.00	441	333	$431	19

Do you know anyone planning on keeping their hybrid an extra 20 to 40 years when they buy one? I don't. Here is a little table that will make you the resident expert and storyteller on the matter at your next Sunday barbecue.

TABLE 20: **Driving Distances Required in Order to Financially Justify Your Hybrid**

Price Per Gallon	Miles To Drive	Starting Point	Destination	Details
$2.00	556,364	Earth	Earth	Circle Moon 36 Times
$2.50	445,091	Earth	Earth	Circle Equator 18 Times
$3.00	370,909	Los Angeles	Beijing	Round Trip 30 Times
$3.50	317,922	Boston	Moscow	Round Trip 35 Times
$4.00	278,182	South Pole	North Pole	Round Trip 6 Times

In fairness, an increase of just 11 MPG across *all* the vehicles in operation would save the American public some 35 billion gallons of gasoline per year. But to achieve this goal, we need to have affordable technology, not just technology. Folks having purchased hybrids thus far have done so out of the kindness of their hearts, not because it ever made sound financial sense.

In fact, hybrids have made no financial sense to consumers whatsoever. In order to support the price differential to buy a hybrid, let's look at an average consumer. If he owns the vehicle for three years and drives it 45,000 miles, he will save 323 gallons of gas over his entire ownership experience. Those extra gallons would have to be priced at $25 apiece to justify the expenditure. At that rate, a driver of a standard Civic could throw a quarter out his window every mile-and-a-half of driving and still not equal the price differential of a hybrid.

The automaker that can marry the ecological green to affordable green will make a ton of green. Does the government think automakers don't know this? That perhaps this infinitesimal little factoid has somehow eluded their radar screen? Please. Government, if you believe big businesses such as the automakers are as greedy as you say they are, they know all about fuel prices influencing their business. They know all about achieving the holy grail of capitalism right now—achieving iconic pop culture green-god status.

All the financial glory will be gained by marketing *affordable* alternative fuel technology. So if government wants to get these things done, then it must simply get out of the way. Stop your union pandering, market manipulation, and insanely complicated and unnecessary regulation—beginning with CAFE standards.

Securities, Commodities & Currency Manipulation
(It's Not Just for Breakfast Anymore)

While the government can't seem to keep its hands off of labor, technology, market demand, and marketable securities valuations—and doing a deplorable job with all that, I might add—they have recently become enamored with commodity stabilization.

What do I mean? The government intends to put a floor on gas prices by taxing it while it's cheap. This means gasoline can't become too reasonable, or government will step in and raise the price. These same Einsteins, by the way, refused to charge a windfall tax on record-breaking oil company revenues during the days of $4.11 per gallon gas prices. Now, apparently, the bright idea is to tax citizens—fortunate to still have a job to drive to—as they commute back and forth to work.

In the People's Republic of Massachusetts, Governor Deval Patrick is attempting to raise his gas tax an additional $.19 per gallon. The increase would take the state's gas tax to $.61 per gallon, the highest in the nation. I am sure our fine governor will remove some of that tax when the Feds get around to enacting Cap and Trade taxes. Sure. Furthermore, his plan is to place chips in vehicle state inspection stickers—tracking drivers—and taxing them on the basis of Massachusetts road use. Egads!

The cake-taker to all of this is the virtually complete socialization of the auto industry. Perhaps my next book will be entitled *Kremlin Wreck*. As I watch, hear, and read these government initiatives, I am almost desensitized to the transformation of what used to be considered a lot of money. Katherine Wellington, a trusted Massachusetts real estate developer, recently asked me, "Do you remember when numbers used to start with the letter M? We traded them for Bs in 2008. It looks like 2009 is the year of the T!" Her point is well taken: millions, billions, trillions. . . .

The principles of supply and demand apply to monetary supply as well as vehicles. Too much money in the system means too much will be spent later on down the road when folks are more confident. All this spending (increased demand) will drive the supply of goods and services downward, raising prices uncontrollably. The government will be forced to pull back much of the capital it has printed and borrowed in order to fund the TARP, stimulus, and omnibus programs.

The manner in which it goes about this task will be to raise the rates on Treasury Bills; thereby enticing you to stop spending and start investing in government bonds. Everybody offering bonds will be in the same competitive game too; raising rates to entice you to invest. Interest rates will rise, such as those on home mortgages and car loans. This of course, reduces demand and breaks inflation, but it puts us back into a recession. Tossing billions of dollars at a failing economy is not free. It causes problems for our future.

Out of the $787 billion stimulus bill passed in February 2009, the car industry essentially received no stimulus whatsoever. At the outset, there was a proposal for car buyers to receive a tax deduction for vehicle loan interest. That was removed. Instead, car buyers are only eligible to deduct their state sales tax and town excise tax bills from their net reported income. Well, that amounts to about $1,500 in deductions, translating into roughly $500 in tax savings. Big deal. That's basically one or two monthly car payments. If factory $5,000 rebates aren't stimulating sales, what made these brain surgeons believe a cruddy $500 tax break is going to move the needle?

Cash For Clunkers: The Federal Government Learns about Rebates, Socio-Economic Prejudice, and More Dealership Bankruptcies

Have no fear, the $1 billion (now $3 billion) Cash for Clunkers program is here. Meaning, one can earn government rebates by trading in (and scrapping or junking) an old gas-guzzling, carbon-emitting vehicle. Similar to the GM and Chrysler buyouts, the government is interested in stimulating auto sales only when it advances a political agenda.

Rather than offering federal income tax deductions for vehicle purchases, which would be far easier to administer through run-of-the-mill tax returns, the government enacted a very complicated system of rebates. Why? Because 40% of Americans pay no federal income tax whatsoever. Allowing tax deductions would have simply ingratiated the rich, according to Obama's outlook.

Additionally, new automobile purchases with a price-tag above $49,000 were made ineligible. Trading your clunker for a Cadillac got you no help, even though your tax money was used to both buy GM (for the union) and fund the whole Clunker program for non-taxpayer benefit. The entire premise of a trade-in requirement assumes the car being traded is worth far less than the $3,500 or $4,500 the government is paying you to junk it. The program was clearly focused on the poor. If you made too much money or already drove something worth $4,500 or more, you were out of luck.

The system was so poorly planned and executed that the initial billion dollar budget (designed to last through the third quarter of 2009), was used up in the first two weeks of the program. Dealers offering the $3,500 to $4,500 government-backed rebates were not reimbursed for almost a month after dealers credited the customer this amount and delivered the new car, despite having to *immediately* pay off their floorplan notes to banks in full.

Instead of entrusting the automakers (two of which they now own) with the rebate money administration—a practice they are well equipped and experienced to handle—the government hired Citibank to do the job. Of course, Citibank charges folks interest for a living, rather than administering rebates. So they took some of the $45 billion in taxpayer-funded TARP money they had already received and forked over $19 million to Oracle software company for development of an electronic submission program.

Who runs Oracle software regularly? Do you use Oracle at home? I don't. Neither do *any* car dealers. Paperwork needed to be scanned and uploaded in specific, complicated file formats and name extensions. According to Buddy Irby, a Florida Ford Dealer, on any given day, dealer passwords even failed to work. The program was such a quagmire, NHTSA (National Highway Traffic Safety Administration) extended dealer submission deadlines to accommodate the difficult steps necessary to gain reimbursements.

And at the end of the day, the best-selling model under the program was the Toyota Corolla. Help non-taxpayers with taxpayer money—Check. Waste taxpayer money on goofy administrative guidelines to do so—Check. Help foreign automakers with your money in the process—Checkmate.

If the government could get past the class warfare for a moment, there are far more practical auto industry stimulus solutions. If buyers were allowed to deduct their entire vehicle purchase price from their taxes in the first year or two they buy it, regardless of economic class or product preference, the car business would take off—and so would the economy! Here's the math, assuming an average vehicle MSRP of $26,000 and an average taxpayer federal tax bracket of 30%:

TABLE 21: **A Better Idea from the Start: Tax Credit Stimulus**

New Cars Sold	Aggregate Deductible Spending	Aggregate IRS Credits
12.5 Million	$325 Billion	$97.5 Billion
13 Million	$338 Billion	$101.4 Billion
13.5 Million	$351 Billion	$105.3 Billion
14 Million	$364 Billion	$109.2 Billion
14.5 Million	$377 Billion	$113.1 Billion
15 Million	$390 Billion	$117 Billion
15.5 Million	$403 Billion	$120.9 Billion

$120 billion is a lot of money! At least it used to be. However, considering these credits would have taken just 15% of the entire stimulus bill to implement, and considering one in twelve Americans are employed (directly or indirectly) by the auto industry, the math makes sense. It certainly makes more sense than building a railroad between Los Angeles and Las Vegas with an initial cost of $50 billion, and other less stimulating initiatives in my humble opinion. Heck, we've dropped $63 billion into the industry already and haven't turned things around.

The argument you would hear against my idea is this: car write-offs are just a tax break for the rich. Well, whoever has the money to spend on cars right now is just fine with me. Currently, the lack of excise taxes in Massachusetts is bankrupting towns. My town is currently laying-off 40 high school employees due to necessary budget cuts. Those cuts would be unnecessary if Shrewsbury, Massachusetts and other towns like it were collecting excise taxes on new vehicle registrations.

The towns, counties, states, and our entire nation need to see this industry rise to 15 million units annually. In that environment, most will survive. Not all. Most. Currently we are tracking closer to 9.5 million units. At that level, nobody makes it. Not some. None. What makes the government think that riding the bankruptcies of GM and Chrysler like the *Lone Ranger* is going to get the industry up to this number? Even by President Obama's (perhaps formerly) planned number, the country needs 13 million vehicle sales annually. What does the ownership and control of two automobile companies and annihilation of 2,000 dealers do to sell 3.5 million more cars per year than our last twelve month's pace?

Better to have the $63 billion in federal investment back, cancel projects such as Los Angeles to Las Vegas railroads, free condoms, tattoo removal, and museum endowments to fund a massive auto buyer tax credit. Does it matter who gets the tax benefit when trying to save an entire industry and its employees? No. Perhaps my local teachers can secure a job building railroads or handing out prophylactics. They can jump in line right behind the thousands of United Auto Workers who kept their pensions and healthcare but lost their jobs. If it weren't the government doing it to us, it would be considered a crime. Use your votes like a sword.

Nineteen

How Short-Term Thinking Wrecked the Industry

... and Pummeled Your Wallet

"Wanting isn't the problem. Problems occur when we develop the habit of indulging every want, or wants we cannot afford."

—J.D. ROTH
www.getrichslowly.org

hort-term thinking is a pervasive problem all through the industry and is reflected all across our society, our government, and our culture. Consumers do not delay a purchase until they can really afford a new home. Bankers loan money to buyers who do not qualify with a down payment or sufficient income to pay off the loan. They can secure government and private sector insurance to cover the potential default foreclosures anyway. Government-controlled Fannie Mae, Freddie Mac, and AIG get pummeled, along with their shareholders. When that runs out, the government just forks over more cash to cover the losses—leaving you in the lurch to pay the bills. Our politicians perpetuate this kind of behavior, because granting voters their home-ownership wishes regardless of their financial means is how they get elected!

It appears none of these parties have considered what the long-term impact of their actions might be on you. We seem to be too often driven by immediate bottom-line profits, by greed for money or votes, by the quest for immediate gratification. Much of this is understandable. People want the greatest returns while minimizing risk. Investors have plenty of places to put their money. When expectations go unmet, they pull their money out of one business and find another. This means a business doesn't just desire to make money, it *must* make money. Just watch the single-day fluctuations of many publicly traded companies in the stock market and you can see what I mean.

If one wants to study the purest form of "no-excuses" risk management, look no further than the banking industry. Prior to making a business loan, bankers want both a proven business history and a proforma expectation of future results. After making a loan, credit committees don't give a hoot about the changing business climate or managerial troubles. They simply want the results for which they signed up. When anything falls out of line, such as the profits their borrowers forecasted, they pull the loan, foreclose, and hit the road. Businesses have to make money in order to satisfy lenders, even in the short-term.

Democracy and the free-market economy are the best environments in which to live, work and worship. These freedoms are as fundamental to our American way of life as it gets. When you can't live, work, and worship where and with whomever you like, it feels as if you are missing the carbon, nitrogen, and oxygen we all require as human beings. The price paid for all this freedom is the fickleness of consumers, lenders, and investors that so often accompany it.

Customers have a choice of what they buy and where they buy it. Banks get to make money on virtually any and every one of these consumer choices, charging them interest on their credit cards, vehicle loans, home mortgages, and debit card transactions. Manufacturers and service providers of all types jump into the mix with "financeable" products. Retailers get to set up their tents wherever the manufacturers and government allow them to. And government gets to collect too much of everyone's income, then tell us all what we can do with the rest. But in a democracy, consumers and voters decide who makes it in this game.

We don't have to finance as much or as long. We don't have to buy anyone's particular product or service that doesn't suit us. We don't have to elect politicians who promise to take more of our income or more of our freedoms. We have a say in the process.

The problems inherent with democracy and free markets are indisputable, no doubt. It is a sad fact that greed reigns absent of oversight. This means when the cat is away, the mice will play. Manufacturers take advantage of the dealers, banks, and customers in the name of greed. Dealers take advantage of manufacturers, banks, and customers in the name of greed. Unions and employees take advantage of their employers and the government whenever possible. And quite frankly, banks take advantage of every one of those aforementioned parties in the game.

The government varies and wavers between the productively supportive and outright misguided in the regulation of it all! The definition of right and wrong boil down to the size of campaign contributions. The "free" market goes away when the government rewards bad behavior by selectively and prejudicially saving some businesses while demolishing others. Businesses and products must be allowed to fail, or the system is not free at all.

Since "self-regulation" of industry has proven to be a dismal failure, *some* oversight is needed. However, look who is providing the oversight: Czars appointed by presidents and lacking any legislative oversight whatsoever, cabinet secretaries who don't pay their taxes, and an executive U.S. auto industry task force that is completely unaccountable, much less identifiable. These folks don't give interviews and thus, never get pinned down or challenged on decisions that consume our money and affect our lives. The power grab is a jump ball.

In order to preach and teach self-regulation or impose government regulation, an example of self-control needs to be demonstrated by the policy makers. The $787 billion stimulus and $410 billion omnibus pork-pie bills literally did nothing to spur auto industry sales. Rather, ample funding was made available to fulfill a decades-old program wish-list for politicians. This set an awful example: the unrestrained spending of taxpayer money, borrowing against future tax payments, and printing currency to make up the rest.

There will always be the self-serving and greedy to contend with in any society. In societies offering a free market, greed can be checked by getting rid of short-term thinking at the consumer and voter level—especially the type of thinking that trades financial insanity for corporate campaign contributions and votes. Short-term thinking throws accountability in the wastebasket. We teach and preach a lack of accountability to our kids through our own examples of such behavior. "It's So and So's fault, not mine."

I was raised to expect the government to protect me from the physical harm of criminals and hostile nations. I was not raised to rely on the government to support me financially or dig me out of bad personal or business decisions. When we consumers take the bait of greed, we feed the system with our financial flesh. Alternatively, encouraging the government to legislate consumer common sense is an exercise in killing freedom. Government doesn't even know how to live by its own rules, never mind make up new ones for you and me to follow. It hypocritically grandstands the lack of accountability in others, while perpetually wiggling itself off the hook. Every time I hear a Republican or Democrat talk about fiscal responsibility, I giggle. Then I became angry. How dare they preach tightening our belts as they blow taxpayer money on Air Force One photo opportunities, pet projects, and the interests of political contributors. Would you not agree?

Mr. and Mrs. Consumer, don't allow government to dictate what businesses can and cannot do for you. It limits your choices. Take charge, be aware, and refuse to trade your free choices for consumer protectionism. After all, these government folks enabled the home mortgage mess, failed to restrict the use of billions of dollars in TARP money, rewarded unions for depreciating your vehicle and burying two companies, and allowed banks to tear you apart via the rule of 78s. Do you need more proof that government doesn't know or care what *really* hurts you?

Their job is to get reelected. Your job is to make wise decisions with your money (or what's left of it after taxes). They cannot behold you while simultaneously pandering to the folks who write big campaign checks. They have no interest in protecting you from the companies they now own. They can pretend you're important by passing some baloney laws that look good on the outside. At the end of the day however, perhaps we are all better off on our own, without government intervention.

Short-term thinking will never go away in a democratic society. Consumers will always want what they want, when they want it, regardless of the ramifications. Furthermore, there will always be someone willing to feed that appetite for a profit. Government's removal of those enablers only removes consumer choice, freedom, and democracy. No, the only true check on greed, which still preserves our freedom, is personal accountability and individual responsibility.

This means consumers must inform themselves, calculate the implications of their intended action, and at times restrain themselves. When they make mistakes, the burden is theirs to bear, not the innocent taxpayer. Teaching accountability is impossible when somebody else is bailing you out of the consequences. Personal control is tantamount. Lessons are inevitable.

Short-term thinking and its associated greed are incredibly pervasive in our American culture, but these seem insignificant compared to the lack of personal accountability. Folks find reasons to justify almost any behavior. Theft, infidelity, even murder are seemingly justifiable in the mind of the guilty. These days, one person's indiscretion—in addition to inevitably becoming another person's problem—is yet a third person's fault. Folks generally do whatever they want, regardless of the consequences to themselves or others. Once heralded to account, they back-fill the actions with a litany of excuses. That's human nature.

In the end, just as I have personally found no solace in the judicial system to fix human nature, you the consumers will find none in the legislative system—none that doesn't strip you of your choices. Instead, do business like a long-term thinker. Take a look at what your car is likely to be worth a few years down the line *before* you buy it. Bite the bullet on your negative-equity problem. Either remedy it with cash or take a shorter term and higher payment in order to catch up. If you can't afford the payment, buy something less expensive, or wait to buy something until the time is right. Do something right, rather than wait for the right thing to happen. Battle greed with the power of personal discernment. Be different. Be accountable.

Twenty

The Future of the U.S. Auto Industry

... A DeLorean with a Flux Capacitor

"The past is of no importance. The present is of no importance. It is with the future that we have to deal. For the past is what man should not have been. The present is what man ought not to be. The future is what artists are."

—OSCAR WILDE
Poet & Thespian (1854–1900)

The year is 2014, and this is how the U.S. Auto Industry looks today:

The result of federal government and union ownership of Chrysler and GM has bled the American taxpayer some $40 billion per year for the first five years of ownership. The number is skewed. It has been understated by the removal of employee healthcare expenses into a government/taxpayer-funded healthcare system. Despite removal of this tremendous burden off the backs of the corporations and onto taxpayers, they still cannot turn a profit.

Enabled by biased and predatory government subsidies, both GM and Chrysler now market green cars at a price well below Ford and other competitors. Including the initial investment of $60 billion into GM, GMAC, Chrysler, and Chrysler Credit Corp., the government has invested a total of $300 billion into these companies, in order to keep them afloat. Failing to turn the automakers around, Congress and the executive branch have hired and fired senior management several times. Each new regime's replacement was vetted through Congressional hearings.

Talented CEOs don't want to work for the government-owned automakers. Regulations now govern all compensation plans and there is little financial reward in being among the next round of highly publicized terminations. The adverse personalized media coverage and personal attacks levied by dissenting government overseers—attempting to dictate corporate policy and rustle votes—is a no-win proposition. Political appointees having little experience or talent, but falling under cover of the governing party now run the companies.

Manipulation of the federal domestic tax code and new agency regulations give GM and Chrysler an economic advantage. Passage of Card Check legislation (billed as "the Employee Freedom of Choice Act") further harasses car companies in competition with the government. Senator Al Franken's confirmation empowered the fil-ibuster-proof 2009–2010 Senate majority into passing the bill with little debate. Unionization of virtually all auto manufacturers, ven-dors, suppliers, and dealerships began prior to the 2010 mid-term elections.

Businesses are distracted by massive waves of union collective bargaining and mandatory government intervention into pay plans, benefits, and work conditions. The NLRB has gone on a hiring spree throughout the nation in order to keep up with the new demands of government-written employer agreements. Most of the new hires emanate from unions, community organizations, and other politically connected entities. Few, if any, have ever operated a business, but are happy getting paid to tell others how to run theirs.

Chinese and Indian automakers are quick to take advantage of the U.S. automakers' resulting competitive disadvantage. The President attempted to include an import tariff, in order to dissuade further Asian entries into the U.S. market. China objected due to the

$1 trillion in U.S. debt owned or backed by its government. India leveraged destabilization of its region via pressure on Pakistan, a country with its hands full. The entire import tariff initiative was shot down.

Consequently, Korean and Japanese automakers, regardless of ample manufacturing capabilities here, dumped product by the thousands on U.S. markets. The vehicles have far less demand overseas and were imported here on the cheap due to their lower foreign labor costs, and ample dealer networks still operating profitably in the U.S.

Under government control, GM and Chrysler have terminated 5,000 dealerships. Most of these business locations have been developed for alternate uses. Remaining dealers, in good retail locations, began voluntary termination of their franchise agreements in order to form new alliances with Chinese and Indian automakers entering the U.S. market. Korean and Japanese automakers received an automatic expansion of dealership locations via candidates waiting franchise-less in the wings. Other dealers retaining GM and Chrysler franchises are rapidly attempting to fly the American coop, however.

There are civil court cases brought by automakers against their dealers in all fifty states. They are attempting to enforce site-control agreements prohibiting dealers from changing franchises. Such agreements were signed by many dealers as a condition of receiving "free" franchises—seized from competing dealers—during GM and Chrysler's structured bankruptcies. Dealers argue that the government did not keep its end of the bargain. Those trying to switch brands are audited mercilessly and starved of any models that are still selling.

GM and Chrysler dealers still struggle to make money. There is far more profit in representing a competitor. The President continues to label such moves as "Un-American." Nobody buys into the rhetoric. He ordered the Small Business Administration (SBA) to stop the guarantee of dealer floorplan other than in Chrysler and GM dealerships. The move is designed to curb dealer defection plans via government control over most floorplan-providing banks. All banks under federal control now deny credit to dealers other than GM and

Chrysler. These car companies continue to hemorrhage cash and blame their dealer network, which has grown smaller and weaker each year. Competing automakers become more aggressive with captive finance companies in order to provide dealer floorplan and customer auto loans.

Many of the banks have been nationalized. Private sector investors were not interested in purchasing "toxic" home-mortgage assets from the banks, leaving lenders unable to provide loans. Anybody contemplating doing business in partnership with the government, "went to school" over the front-page exposure of AIG bonus recipients, protests held by ACORN on their front lawns, and predatory bonus taxes passed by Congress in 2009. Nobody trusted the federal government sufficiently in order to partner with it in purchasing toxic assets from the banks. They were afraid that making money in partnership with the government would be vilified and taxed as a means to impress angry taxpayers. But the banks could not lend with the toxic assets on the books. So the government purchased the assets in exchange for common stock in the banks—gaining management control.

Conservative political groups call for the government to return these banks to the private sector. Congressman Barney Frank (D–MA) and others like him are drunk with the power of it all. Bank nationalization allows prejudicial treatment of certain individuals and industries suiting the government's political ideology and campaign funding. Everybody else has trouble getting a loan and the economy suffers for it.

Asian imports have grown to represent over 70% of the domestic U.S. market. Less than three in ten sales occurs in a Ford, Chrysler, or GM dealership. Ford resurrected its leasing program, joining the Asian brands in its assault to raise residual values. GM and Chrysler continue to sell automobiles to fleet and rental companies in order to keep their union owners earning wages—despite the consequences. This keeps the union working but kills residual resale values. The government guarantees buybacks from fleet customers under their "Believe in American Products" campaign.

Consequently, the market continues to be flooded with current model year and one-year-old used cars, leaving the remaining privately-held lenders (fortunate to have paid back their TARP money), reluctant to write auto loans on government products. Only banks under TARP influence still write auto loans on their vehicles. The government is fully subsidizing these companies. They pay to build, rebate, buy back and finance everything—and lose taxpayer money by doing so.

Depressed residuals have forced the government out of leasing its own products. It attempts to collect on established AIG residual value insurance policies it forced the company to write in exchange for its TARP investments. Since no lock-box reserve had been set up in order to back these policies, another political scandal ensues. AIG's residual insurance liability created further insolvency for the company, which still suffers from a severe talent shortage due to government-controlled pay plans. Special House appropriations were then necessary to fund off-lease vehicle losses, and to continue propping up AIG.

TALF and private investors refuse to invest in toxic lease portfolios including GM and Chrysler products. Based upon the (government regulated and controlled) miscalculation of its own products' resale values, the SEC labels *all* lease portfolios as toxic. Thus anyone having made investments in securitizing lease portfolios is now stuck, unable to leverage them on the market at a fair value. This cuts off the money supply, hamstringing both Ford and the imports from leasing, regardless of their lease portfolio's stellar performance. Like all predatory policies designed to protect government-owned companies, this was used as a means of hobbling the competition further.

Liberal media are no longer able to bury these stories. Taxpayers are objecting by participating in elections in which "what to do about the auto company crisis" is a central political issue. The government responds with plans to transfer the remaining common share ownership of the companies to the UAW in exchange for preferred stock. The move riddles the *new* automakers with debt, but it promises a means to cease further taxpayer capital investment. Having assumed liability for the companies' pensions and healthcare, the government otherwise extricated itself from further overt involvement or support.

On the contrary, the Canadian government initially retained its common stock stake in General Motors in exchange for temporary union wage freezes. No matter. The UAW bled the companies dry and filed for liquidation under Chapter 7 bankruptcy code. Prior to the filing, the Italians at Fiat determined they were no more clever than the two American and one German management groups who have failed with the company. They turn in their 20% share of Chrysler to the union in exchange for commitments to import and resell Fiats to U.S. rental car companies.

On the way out, the federal government insists preferred share-holders are prioritized in the bankruptcy. Unlike the shenanigans of the structured bankruptcies of 2009, the shoe is on the other foot. The federal write-off of billions of dollars in stock losses are too much for taxpayers to bear quietly.

As of August 2009, these future events appear evident to me. Unless an extreme change occurs, of course. I do not believe the U.S. Supreme Court would uphold an argument that the government's program is illegal. Whether secured creditors and dealers each file suit is beyond my prediction. However, GM ditched $100 billion in debts and liabilities without so much as one creditor coming out whole on the plan. Consumers, taxpayers, private investors—you—got rear-ended, run over, and crushed in the *Car Wreck* of it all.

I did not pull the problems of the industry out of thin air. They are real. They are true to form. I did not simply Google "describe and fix all things about the auto industry" and present the findings here. That strategy would have been a lot easier for me, if such information had ever existed before this book.

I concluded a recent trip by speaking with a man on a flight from JFK to Logan. As I worked on a hard copy of this manuscript, we naturally began talking about the car business.

"It sounds like you've studied the business a lot," he said.

"No, sir," I replied. "I lived it."

Thank-you for reading my book. Take a look at my appendices. I have provided some industry fixes and the influences from where my perspective comes. Visit me at www.CarDealerLife.com or www.MarkRagsdale.com to learn more about up-to-date rear-endings and what you can do to protect yourself.

ACKNOWLEDGMENTS

Writing this book has been a wonderfully challenging experience. My loving family supported, for the most part, the all-nighters required to complete the project. However, my son, Wyatt, did hold me to midnight bedtimes from time to time. I also received well-wishes and blessings from many friends and colleagues to whom I am grateful.

My eternal love and gratitude to my amazing wife, Lauri, who has endured the countless emotional roller-coaster rides inherent with the car business. She is also my warmest critic. The eleventh-hour marathon final editing sessions we pulled off together made this book!

My love and wonder for our two beautiful children, Wyatt and Isabella, who provide me with unconditional love, regardless of the frustrated expressions Daddy had on his face from time to time during the project.

Love, thanks, and honor to my parents George and Beverly Ragsdale, who provided me an education, a financial head start, and parental love and guidance that I enjoy to this day.

To my in-laws, Bob and Mary Ann Avolizi, many thanks for your love and support. You are all wonderful models for our children.

To my editor, Diane Solomon, who organized a navigable forest out of the chapters of trees I flung at her throughout the writing process. Without her, *Car Wreck* would have been nothing more than a series of isolated rants.

To the employees of Langdon Street Press, for their patience and encouragement.

To Kathy Smith for creating the book's subtitle.

To Del LeMond and Barry Kerrigan of Desktop Miracles for both superior interior and cover designs.

To Dottie DeHart of DeHart and Company, my publicist, for keeping the word out on me and my work.

To the former employees of Ragsdale Motor Group—300 strong—especially Rob Baker, Terry Bush, Brenda Bouvier, Kimberly Kennedy, Barbara Reynolds, Tonia Smith, Paula Stafinski, Charlene White, Scott Chase, Dean Lemovitz, Glen Reed, Paul Bernard, Colleen Letendre, and Buddy Irby. Your warm hearts and hard work are a beacon of example to anyone working in the car industry today.

To Bob Recore, for his tireless pragmatism as acting COO of Ragsdale Motor Group while we wound down operations in 2008.

To Peter "Zip" Zipfel of Creative Electronic Media, Gary Green of Gary L. Green Marketing, and Charlie Perry and his team at C. Perry and Associates, who have become my friends and partners in helping dealers with their challenges today.

To Grant Cardone and Scott Morgan of Cardone Enterprises, as well as Marc Smith of Marc Smith International for their sales training throughout the last decade of my career.

To Bob O'Koniewski Esq., Executive Vice-President of MSADA, for sharing vital legislative content and insight.

To Abbas Qutab M.D., President of Elan Vital, and Rob Rossetti, President of Northeast Seminars, for getting me off the ground and keeping me going.

To Mitz Qutab, Tim Valentijn, Steve O'Neill, Terry Condon, Lisa Abraham, Linda Knight, Owen Blevins, Larry Glick, Traci Fleischman, Pete Paldino, and Kris Koss, D.V.M., Cindy Weir, and Mark and Karyn Wagner, for the finest early manuscript analysis of the work I could ever imagine.

To John Lajoie of Lajoie Investigations, a published author and friend, for guidance in writing style and direction regarding an author's role in book marketing.

To my brothers at NADA 20-Group KI-01, for smacking me upside the back of my head when needed and honoring me with the Chairmanship post. We shared some tremendous times of glory and sorrow together. I miss you all.

And especially to Dave and Pam Penttila, as well as Pastor William and Kathy McKinnon, for taking an interest in my personal relationship with God.

"Jesus, come into my heart, which I open up to you.
I repent of all my sins, both known and unknown. Amen."

Appendixes

A

Industry Fixes for Industry Pros
...and Informed Consumers

*"It is more honorable to repair a
wrong than to persist in it."*
—THOMAS JEFFERSON
Third U.S. President & Author of the
Declaration of Independence (1743–1826)

Corrective Actions for Automakers

Automakers must make a radical change in planning and priorities in order to prepare their businesses for the new global financial oversight model the administration is conceding to. You will not be able to remain in business if you don't respond appropriately, as evidenced by what is going on in the industry today. Toyota is a well-run player, yet it still manages to lose billions in today's market. Here are some fundamental items to address.

Automakers: Require All Automaker District Managers to Graduate from NADA Dealer Candidate Academy (DCA)

Pick some level of management above which you will not promote anyone who has not graduated from the NADA Dealer Candidate Academy. If you implement the decision to only promote NADA

Academy graduates, your people will have a full understanding of your very complex financial statement. Most importantly of all, your people will learn what it takes to be a car dealer. At least when they try to help with operational ideas, they will know their knee-cap from a ball-cap.

If you really want to sell more cars to happier customers, you must learn the business by getting closer to the consumer. This cannot be accomplished through focus groups. You must regain the trust and respect of your only customer—your dealers. They will lead you to the right answers as they deal with the real questions and concerns of the end-user on a day-to-day basis.

Automakers: Prioritize Your Dealers' Profitability

You must agree and support the immutable fact that dealer profitability is tantamount to customer satisfaction. In fact, if you cannot or will not agree that your dealers must be profitable, there is no good reason for you to read any further. Forget about the rest of the fixes. First and foremost, dealers must make money. Period.

You want your "retail" customers to shop their products in conveniently located, well lit, spatial, brand-specific facilities. Who wouldn't? But you often put the cart before the horse. You seem to feel if the dealer puts it all on the line to build one of these dealerships, they will sell more cars. I heard some twenty years ago at a NADA conference that when a dealer builds a huge, successful dealership facility—they call it his *monument*. But if it fails, they call it his *mausoleum*, because he buried himself in it. No doubt, if trendy upscale dealerships are your thing, who would blame you. You are right. But it is just plain arrogant to expect this without helping dealers to sell more cars *and* make more money in order to justify the financial risk.

And of course, profitable dealers that have substantial enough market potential will build you a slew of customer amenities at their dealerships. I've seen restaurants, golf putting courses, simulators, movie theaters, day cares, and spas inside dealerships! These special little niceties take a lot of investment as well as a lot of focus and a bunch of dealership revenue to support. If you want these things in your stores, help your dealers to become more profitable.

Automakers: Stop Taking Dealer Money

Manufacturers have dozens of ways to pilfer a dealer's profits and cash flow. I'm sorry to have to use the word "pilfer," but I honestly cannot think of another that is more appropriate. Get some control over your budgets and stop sending and charging dealers for stuff that is *your* responsibility.

Dealers fund billions in Dealership Marketing Group (DMG) funds. Don't you think you can pony up with updated product merchandising material? Heck, even my radio stations gave me free t-shirts, pens and mugs. You ship your dealers all kinds of items: tools, posters, brochures, announcement banners, and the list goes on and on. Your dealers have absolutely no control over what shows up on their doorstep and even less when you take the money out of their accounts to pay for it all. What other business can you think of that has its hands in the pockets, literally, of its distributors?

Audits are killers. Suffice it to say, they are a miserable way to punish dealers—intentional or not. You have to ask yourself in a very unemotional way "Is getting what I believe I can get back worth the consequences to my company?" Five to ten percent warranty cost overages are a pittance compared to the money that is wasted in your company right now. At least this one ensures proper care of your customers.

Moreover, if you really got down to brass tacks, you save 25% on warranty labor and 30% on warranty parts already—via your labor time guides and mandatory parts discount programs. The parts you charge back are essentially free to you, because dealers buy them from you and pay you a profit up front for them! I'm talking about little or no skin off your nose to make this change. A change designed to better care for both your wholesale and retail customers. Legitimate fraud is the obvious exception. However, we both know, as do the readers of this book, that audits are used outside of this purpose.

Do you need proof? In the history of your employment with the automaker, how many dealer fraud cases can you remember? And what was the percentage of such cases relative to the total number of dealer audits you have conjured? Are the two-percenters worth disturbing your dealer network's focus on customer sales & satisfaction? I hope so, because this is what your audits are yielding right now across America. Retail customers peeved in the service lane don't just find another one of your dealers. They leave your brand altogether.

Automakers: Be Willing To Pay For What You Want

When you pay dealers for what you want, they do it. When you expect it for nothing, they resent you. You are not in business to do something for nothing. What makes you think dealers don't share this profit motive with you?

Somebody gave you a job, and somebody else gave him a personally guaranteed loan to make his own troubles. You risk losing your job. He risks losing his business, his home and anything else the bank wanted to grab from him as collateral. Your dealer expects and deserves compensation for his risk and associated efforts.

Some manufacturers, such as Suzuki and Kia, pay for what they want. They are a step ahead of you in that regard. Most times, when you assume you are paying for what you want, three common mistakes get you into trouble and the program fails:

Unreasonable Objectives: Often, a dealer cannot compete within the group he is placed. I remember being asked to buy into a program by purchasing 80 more vehicles from the factory. Their rationale: since I did such a great job selling cars in October, the factory would just double my orders. All the guys doing a cruddy sales job in October had to purchase and carry the interest on *fewer* vehicles in order to participate. I was essentially being punished for doing a good job.

Paying the incentive too slowly: After program completion, pay right away. Everyone likes immediate gratification. Likewise everyone has heard or used the old line; "The check is in the mail." I did my best to pass out cash incentives to my salespeople immediately. Deliver a car, get the green cash. The amounts were reported and payroll withholding was deducted from the recipient's next weekly paycheck. I referred to these incentives as "WDK" (Wife Don't Know) money, breaking my own rule of "nothing good comes from acronyms." Spouses look at the net paycheck after all mandatory and elective withholdings. Taxes paid on an extra hundred or two in compensation "spiff" money was never detected. More of this and less of "the check is in the mail" mentality from you will go a long way in improving your contests.

Funding the program by stealing the incentive money from some other (successful) program: Dealers take wild risks to move cars during your programs. They lose money on car deals, pay too much for customer trade-ins just to make the incentive money, and in general, make quick ratification to their operating philosophy. The least you can do is pay them what they've earned and do so quickly. However, taking a dealer's money out of one of his pockets and placing it in another is a terribly demotivating and transparent offense.

Automakers: Control Your Production Rather than Bury Your Dealer in Inventory!

You must do the math before asking a dealer to take unnecessary surplus inventory. It is not okay to coerce dealers into stocking cars they do not need. Let your conscience guide you, even when your boss(es) are on your butt to move cars. It is short-sighted on your part to swamp a dealer with inventory. If he fails—and too much inventory is the biggest killer of them all—how does this help you to sell cars? You will be buying them back from the defunct dealer and shuffling them off to another dealership that probably doesn't need them either. Regardless of what the government Wall Street whiz kids say, firing a self-funded and self-motivated sales force is dumb. Putting one out of business because you can't calculate stocking requirements on the back of a napkin is downright asinine.

Automakers: Reduce or Eliminate Rental Company/Fleet Sales

Immediately cease or radically reduce fleet sales! You need to provide only the minimum needed for product exposure. I'm talking about getting control of your fleet subsidy budgets as well as your residual values so you can lease cars profitably by selling more vehicles more often to more customers.

Honda began an advertising campaign in March 2009 that touted their superior residual values. That's essentially the whole ad; touting residual values. They claim their superior residual values allow them to have the best leases and finance rates. Are you stupid enough to argue with them? I hope not. Because they are correct. Moreover, they didn't earn that title by overproducing, then bending over and taking it from fleet companies, did they?

Now I know this is easier said than done. For many years fleet sales have been a convenient way for manufacturers to solve failed retail sales and production models. To do this, you must be able to predict the market. The reason you cannot accurately predict the market today stems from your vehicle's massive depreciation schedules and the effect it has on consumer auto lenders approving loans.

To predict the market, you must be able to calculate the point in time when the retail customer *has* to make a decision, rather than when he *wants* to make a decision. You have the ability to drive this concept home through leasing, provided you get control of your residual values. You must get out of selling cars to rental companies in order to control your residual values and offer viable leases. You must restore faith in the banking and residual value insurance carriers to believe in your products.

Automakers: Quit Offering Rebates and Replace Them with Affordable Upside-down Aid for Consumers

Traditionally, you have carved up your marketing budgets into three buckets: advertising/promotion, rebates/financing incentives, and fleet discounts/buybacks. The fix involves abating and eventually eradicating the last two buckets: rebates/financing incentives and fleet discounts/buybacks. Let's call these last two marketing expenses the Z Buckets. They are the most costly last-ditch-efforts to move product.

Furthermore, the Z Buckets dramatically increase the rate of vehicle depreciation, which is the absolute polar opposite of your goal—consumer upside-down aid. Placing money in the Z Buckets, while attempting to minimize consumer negative equity is like a dog chasing its own tail. Every dollar placed in a Z Bucket creates literally double trouble. There is one *less* dollar available for upside-down aid, and ironically, one *more* dollar needed to combat the negative equity you just created. No. The idea is to rapidly reallocate *all* Z Bucket dollars into consumer upside-down aid. We are going to call this aid the A Bucket.

In the past, Z Bucket rebates have served to cajole lenders into using such incentives to hide or bury consumer negative equity. We all know that the only player fooled by this mess was the consumer. Everyone else knew what they were doing. The real problem with Z Bucket mollification of consumer negative equity is the zero sum gain. Meaning, the negative equity still exists, but is just hidden from view for a while. In reality, a $5,000 rebate used to finance a $5,000 negative-equity problem still makes the new vehicle being financed worth—you guessed it—$5,000 less! Therefore, no negative-equity issues were either solved or addressed, outside of playing games with bank lending guidelines. You and I must agree that this is neither a sustainable nor a long-term solution.

Given that the average consumer is $4,700 upside-down, we need to apply sufficient A Bucket money along with a viable consumer finance vehicle, in order to get rid of the problem. Further, we need to see that it never rears its ugly head again. By ditching Z Bucket money, you can far better control your vehicle's rapid depreciation. We all know vehicle depreciation affects residual values, and, residual values are tracked and overseen by the ALG, Automotive

Lease Guides. We further know ALG relies heavily on current used car book values and historical Z Bucket incentives to refine their predictions. ALG is particularly squirrely about fleet-game auction reports and last year's customer rebate numbers. They should be. Aside from the aforementioned brand-damaging cookout stories, these two factors have the greatest impact on depreciation and negative equity.

ALG and lender protection are important, because these are the players you need in order to get your business growing again. Why? 42-month short-term leases are the financial vehicle we are going to use to sell more cars to the same people more often. Why? Your consumer will have a fully paid-up contract, owe nobody, and have nothing to drive, without making a *new* purchase or lease decision every three and a half years.

Even better, consumers can get rid of $4,700 in negative equity during the term of a 42-month lease for approximately $125 extra per month. You can subsidize this negative equity amount with former Z Bucket incentive savings—all without creating additional negative equity!

This is important, so I am going to say it again: *By getting the customer into a shorter contract, fully paid up in three and a half years, owing nobody and thus having no negative equity, both automakers and their dealers sell more cars simply by selling to the same customers more often.*

By taking ownership of the negative-equity epidemic on behalf of your consumers, you will be able to pinpoint sales demand, produce the right amount of cars, and save money on costly incentives.

Corrective Actions for Car Dealers

Automotive retail has hit a new era. There will be far less competition between many same-make dealers in the same market as well as fewer overall dealership locations. This means a greater supply of quality employees to choose from in the marketplace and they will be available at more reasonable wages.

It also indicates an enhanced environment of automaker power and state franchise law anemia. Dealers must become even more vigilant in their efforts to protect their businesses. Here are a few items to focus on. More are available at www.CarDealerLife.com.

Car Dealers: Learn To Say "NO"!

Dealers are the most positive people in the world. However, even though you are professional negotiators and very good at selling things to other people, you are also very easy targets when someone else is selling something to you. You are sharp with Sharpies, but soft sells.

Factory district and zone sales managers who call on you make their living by getting you to capitulate. Often, you make decisions to take cars or sign up for such programs regardless of the program's logical business merits. Dealers, you must always remember that local or regional factory representatives will be transferred to another post, advocating nonsensical programs to their new list of dealers. Nobody will remember you refused cars or failed to sign up for a stupid program that put you in danger of financial failure.

You must learn how to say no to things that are not in your best interest. You must cease doing favors for factory managers and expecting reciprocity when you need them most. You must remain cordial and cooperative with the factory people, which is hard to do, when their business propositions are less than mutually beneficial. But being submissive with inventory control or nonsensical initiatives puts you, the dealer, out of business more quickly than any other single reason.

If borrowing $2 million via extra floorplan line obligations for a 3% annualized return is your bag, go get 'em tiger. Otherwise, in the words of Nancy Reagan; "Just Say No!" Download a free electronic inventory cost/benefit analyzer from: www.CarDealerLife.com

Car Dealers: Establish "Continuous Improvement Teams" (CITs)

Dealers, you often overlook the fact that virtually all of your employees are managers in their own right. They manage their household finances, investment incomes, retirement and tuition budgets. Do you really believe they check all that intelligence at the door when they come to work each day? Of course not! Add this to my favorite key to worker motivation; "you can either tell me *what* you want done or *how* you want it done—not both."

Be firm on your goals. Never negotiate this part of the equation. Then challenge your team to plan and execute *how* the organization will accomplish the goal. You always reserve veto power over the plan. Implementing a plan already commanding an employee mandate is far more profitable than trying to implement something you or your managers came up with. A poor plan executed superbly is far more effective than a superb plan executed poorly.

After all, employees are the ones at ground zero, working the field, as it were. They know the issues at their level better than you. You wouldn't ask a technician how to change floorplan banks would you? What makes you so "smart" (and perhaps even arrogant) that you can dictate how to solve shop problems?

Leverage your employees' intelligence so they can be the ones developing the creative solutions towards achieving *your* goals. Cut down on the rat sessions behind the dumpster by either including or neutralizing the mutterers in your employ. More information on setting up and conducting CITs inexpensively at: www.CarDealerLife.com.

Car Dealers: Pick Your Employees *Carefully*!

You must demand great character in your employees. Frankly, you cannot hire anyone you please, then demand this trait. They must already have it when you bring them aboard. This is easier said than done in situations where your business needs a quick makeover in order to remain solvent. Needless to say, be wary of the candidate who moves around frequently and has a Dickens story for every move. Unfortunately, many of these folks are scary talented and very tempting to hire. Most will end up biting you in the butt because "they always leave the way they came in."

This is especially dangerous in the case of key leadership positions. Their makeover will include a changeover of most of your staff, including long-term employees who are loyal to you. They will be quickly replaced by strangers who are loyal to the person who brought them in. When he leaves the way he came in, they will too—all at once—leaving your store empty. The drastic reduction in dealerships will open doors to more available employees, allowing you to make better character choices.

Roving Sage salespeople—with an *alleged* customer following—usually spend more time spreading cancer behind the dumpster, than they do contacting their owner base they bragged about when you hired them. These people demand more guarantees, more commissions, and ultimately perform below the national average. They are great at ratting out your otherwise happy and productive employees, though.

After wreaking havoc on dealership morale, they usually migrate on, plugging their umbilical cord into the next dealer down the street. Don't be surprised if they do so, while towing out a young impressionable whipper-snapper salesperson you had great hopes for. The amount of business this six or eight car-a-month bloviator creates isn't worth the pain, aggravation and brain damage.

Dealers, if you have read this book up to this point, I would like to establish a personal relationship with you. Please send an email to CarWreck@CarDealerLife.com. Be sure to type "I'm a dealer" in the subject line. Please include your best daytime and evening numbers in the body of the email, so I can call you.

Corrective Actions For Government

What can I say to you folks: there are more dealership workers than UAW members? Everybody knows what master you serve. However, unless there is something in it for you by way of campaign contributions or a voting-block, I reckon you will do the right thing. At least considering your lack of any real employment outside of government I mean.

Government: Prioritize the Free Sales Force You Have in Your Dealerships

Without dealers, the automakers have no chance, because they have no ability to sell what they build. Like the rest of the mistakes made when shelling off money in a frantic emergency, automakers historically do not draw this connection. Instead, they blame their dealer networks for the sins they have committed.

As you are giving them money in exchange for board seats, don't be taken in by their red-herring mantra. Don't allow them to use taxpayer money to carry out anti-dealer theories and political dealer hit lists. Take care of the only class of people that can and will sell vehicles through self-motivation and preservation—your dealers.

The folks you sit at the table with have never sold anything to anybody except dealers. And at that, the job never required any salesmanship at all anyway. Many are simply arrogant intimidators willing to blame anyone but themselves for the mess they are in. When dealing with tall children such as these, I caution you to always act like the adult.

Government: Provide Meaningful Stimulus or Get Out of the Way of Necessary Failure

The industry must deliver 15 million units annually in order to survive. Even considering President Obama's 13 million-unit goal, we are only pacing at 9.5 million units annually. What are you going to do about

that? Do you think GM and Chrysler are going to make up that difference under your tutelage? I don't see you addressing the issue. I don't
see the media covering the issue. I see no plan besides cutting dealers and incentivizing the poor (those who drive cars worth less than
$4,500) through tedious government rebate programs. Unfortunately,
the rich, as you define them, must come out and buy as well.

You can continue to put your head in the sand about all the other
red herrings that have led up to where we are today. But banks and
unions—despite their tremendous campaign contributions—have
crushed the industry. And you are ingratiating them with the money
of those "rich" taxpayers you disdain. The provision of consumer tax
credits—substantial ones *outside* of the political class-warfare in vogue
today—are the only way out of this mess.

The raw tax credit number for buyers writing-off their vehicles in
the first year will cost $120 billion. Your non-partisan Congressional
Budget Office can verify this and calculate the *net* cost. Not only will
this strategy put enough cars on the road to keep the industry solvent; it also saves on trickle-down unemployment benefits as well.
Furthermore, employed folks bring in more tax collections than those
who are unemployed. So the real net number is probably closer to $60
billion—the equivalent of all the government has invested so far in
companies it is ill-equipped to run!

Government: Incentivize Short-term Finance Through Leasing

Your first loss is your best loss. Get out of the ownership game and do
something that truly will stimulate the industry. Your current strategy
is a growing waste of federal resources.

Instead, incentivize leasing through capital investment tax credits. Leasing is the only way to protect consumers' vehicle depreciation,
debt, and credit rating. Right now it is a risky proposition for the necessary players to put such a program into place. Make it easy for them.
If you want consumers in the most green technology possible, help
get them behind the wheel of the latest emerging technology—every

three and a half years—without carrying all that nasty upside-down debt into new loan commitments.

Government: Address Mark-to-Market Accounting in a Meaningful Way

Take the mark-to-market accounting rule off the books in its current form. You cannot combat a lie with taxpayer-funded TARP money. A bank holding good-paying mortgage assets should not be punished for Countrywide Financial, Fannie Mae, or Freddie Mac indiscretions. Instead, they should be rewarded with the solid equity and lending ability they have earned. Holding an entire market to the same candle as Anthony Mozilo, Franklin Raines, and Richard Syron is like preaching to the choir.

You can fix the paper shrew you have created with a bottle of white-out. Otherwise, see if members of Congress might consider personally guaranteeing credit arrangements for the dealers in their districts. No? You get the point.

Corrective Actions for Consumers

You drive the whole bus—metaphorically speaking. Meaning, nothing happens until a car gets sold, and you have to buy one in order for that to happen. Here is a quick review of the ways you can and must protect yourself. More information is available at www.MarkRagsdale.com

Consumers: Know the Basics

80% of all car deals involve financing. Financing contingencies consist of:

1. The total amount you are financing relative to the outstanding debt you have on mortgages, other cars, and revolving lines of credit such as credit cards.

2. The total amount being financed on the newer car, relative to the bank's calculation of its wholesale value. This is derived from its original invoice in the case of a brand new or current model year used car, or the (NADA, Kelly Blue Book and Black Book etc.) book values in the case of an older used car.

3. Your credit score as determined by the three credit-scoring services. Also taken into account is the lender's own internal scoring system, which may include knowing you are slow to pay on some things, but faithful as the rising sun with others.

Consumers: Know a few Important Facts about your Individual Situation

Know The True ACV of your Trade-in: The internet, library, and even your insurance agent can get you relevant information quickly. The same books utilized by lenders to calculate your *next* vehicle's loan value are used by dealers as a basis for your *current* vehicle's appraisal. Know the range of these numbers before discounts and rebates get added on at the dealership which gives you a confusing "allowance" number that really masks the truth about your equity position.

Know What You Still Owe on Your Car: You need to know the difference between the market value of your present car and its net payoff amount. Do the math. Are you upside-down? By how much?

Know How Much Your Current Negative Equity Will Cost You Per Month If You Roll it Over into the Next Loan: Download a payment calculator template for free on the web. Start by punching in just the difference between what your car is worth and what you currently owe. As you play with the various terms and interest rates, you can see why there has been very little option for you to control your monthly payment without extending the term.

Bite the Bullet: Increasing your finance contract term in order to maintain your same payment is the worst thing you can do to yourself. You are likely to be shown a more expensive automobile than you wanted, particularly if it has enough margin or enough rebate to make the lender comfortable with their collateral position. Beware.

Know How Bankers Operate: Even if the dealer finds you the car you love, at a payment you can handle, the bank may disagree. I often have seen it come down to the point where the loan analyst will agree to the deal, but must extend your finance term to lower your payment. This usually occurs when your monthly payments consume too much of your verifiable monthly income—after all your household debt service.

The Shorter the Better: By extending the term, you get a lower payment, but you pay a heap-load more interest, which is good for the bank and bad for you! Again, beware. It is best to avoid long-term financing altogether. It's that simple! It was never a good idea, will never be a good idea, and frankly, nobody held a gun to your head while you did it in the past. Now you know the truth. Use it to your benefit by changing your personal buying behavior.

Hedge Against Resale Risk: You do not have a crystal ball in order to project whether your vehicle will maintain much of its value or depreciate wildly. You are not alone. Manufacturers can't call it. Banks and dealers can't call it. So no matter what you "buy," nobody can accurately predict what it will be worth. But no matter what, you will pay the price of depreciation via greater negative equity and the interest on the amounts you roll over. Shorter-term finance contracts help mitigate this situation. Leasing puts the issue to rest altogether!

Consumers: Take Control of Your Actions!

Mr. and Mrs. American Consumer, take control. You are not martyrs. You have either misunderstood or overlooked the real game going on here. You are so worried about the profit made by the dealer on your car purchase, you overlook the stuff that really hurts you! Hey, go out and buy one of those negotiating books if you like. Saving money at the dealer level is a good idea too—all the more power to you. But this is not an equitable trade-off for being hammered by the other stuff.

This means you cannot save yourself into getting a good deal. Those of you accepting a payment you can afford, but with complete disregard for the term of your finance contract, end up feeding your financial flesh to the system. Do you understand what I am saying to you? You make the whole thing possible. When I say you, I really mean "we." I buy and finance things too!

Sure, we can whine at the government for not stopping the banks from offering products that hurt us. However, most of us have taken advantage of the system to get what we wanted when we wanted it—a low payment and NO CASH out of pocket—regardless of the term. Like an ostrich, you plugged your head in the sand, enabling yourself to do what you wanted, when you wanted, regardless of the consequences.

I holler at the automakers for not doing the right things to keep your car from depreciating so quickly. I holler at the banks for offering essentially a "mortgage" while charging you onerous interest penalties on a depreciating asset—your car. Nevertheless, at the end of the day, *you* took advantage of the system.

In an environment where you can buy a motor vehicle on virtually any street corner, and you can find a bank willing to loan you all the money to do it, you have to be responsible. Irresponsibility cannot be solved by any law. The law makes no accommodation for buffoonery (although some industry related civil and class-action suits I've seen test this statement).

Do you eat at greasy fast-food restaurants three times a day, every day? No? Why not? Because it is not healthy for you. Do you need the government to pass a law against that? Point made (I hope).

1. Find a way to live with the discipline *not* to put things on credit cards you cannot pay for today.

2. Do not extend your finance terms to fit a payment on a car. Consider another car instead, or wait until you have some cash to fix the problem.

3. Stop thinking short term. Short-term thinking is reactionary. Start thinking long-term. Long-term thinking is revolutionary.

Consumers: Learn About Leasing & Balloon-Note Financing

I submit that you, Mr. and Ms. Consumer, have overlooked the finest financial vehicle to get what you want debt free and ready for a new start every two or three years. This vehicle is known as either leasing or balloon-note financing. But most of you haven't taken advantage of it.

Automakers sponsor lease programs all the time. If you carry negative equity into a lease deal, you can pay it off at a rate ranging from $25 to $50 per month for every $1,000 dollars of old negative equity you roll in. You need good credit to do this and/or a sizable security deposit. Nonetheless, it is the best untapped resource for auto debt reduction in U.S. History. But it starts with you. Review my chapter on leasing again. Get your credit into sufficient shape. Figure out where you are equity-wise. And shop some lease deals on different products.

B

My Influences

"Pray as though everything depended
upon God. Work as though
everything depended upon you."

—SAINT AUGUSTINE OF HIPPO

hy does a car dealer's kid from Massachusetts wear a cowboy hat? I've had a lot of influences.

I was born in Worcester, Massachusetts in 1966. George, my dad, was born in Madison, Missouri in 1939.

My granddad, Otis Ragsdale, made it his business to purchase dilapidated Missouri farmsteads at reduced prices and restore them with the efforts of his five sons. Dad and his brothers labored over the house, outbuildings, fence-lines and coops. They repaired equipment and worked the fields. Once all was back in functioning order, Granddad would sell it, take his profit, and move on to his next investment property.

The Ragsdales kept livestock, mostly for family consumption, but occasionally sold cattle for cash flow purposes. Tractors were used on the farm, but horses were relied upon heavily for drafting and mounted transportation. Two chickens were slaughtered and dressed for dinner daily. The two-chicken budget was to feed five growing boys, one girl, and two adults. Speed eating was the key to getting oneself a second helping in Granddad's house. Even in his adulthood, it is difficult for my dad to break this habit and eat more slowly.

Dad never had a toilet in the house until he was fourteen. They all trudged through snow and mud just for the pleasure of relieving themselves over a frigid hole in the ground. And on those 100 degree Missouri summer days, they dumped in lime to keep down the stench and flies. The worst job on the farm was rotating the location of that outhouse during the summertime.

As sweltering as Missouri summers can be, the winters are frigid and harsh. The Ragsdales didn't have heat to the second floor bedrooms. For warmth, they would lay bricks on the downstairs stovetop until hot, wrap them in blankets and stuff them at the foot of their shared beds. A drinking glass of water left by the bedside would freeze solid by morning.

Short of high school sports, hunting and fishing were the major rural Missouri pastimes. Some of these enjoyments are illegal today. For example, my family would stretch "taut" lines (a long series of weighted and baited fish hooks) along sections of riverbank, and leave them unattended overnight. They'd "rock fish", an equivalent to modern-day noodling, which by most standards, isn't really *fishing* at all. The idea was to block the entrance-hole of a female catfish's nest, often found between rocks or under a submerged log. This left her but one way out. Dad and his brothers would cajole the now angry cat into biting their hand and wrist. By clamping her gills with proper placement of their thumb, she would go rigid as a board, and could be dragged from the river to the dinner table.

These "river cats" weighed in excess of 35 pounds and hurt when they bit. There are stories of much larger fish drowning noodlers. Dad tells of one burly cat that barreled out of her nest prematurely and knocked the wind clean out of him.

My visits to Missouri were filled with outdoor activities, although I was never old enough or big enough to rock fish while it was still practiced. Granddad, Dad and I would seine hundreds of crayfish ("Crawdads" in Missouri lingo) from designated muddy ponds on the farm. We'd fish them off the banks of clean irrigation ponds stocked with hungry largemouth bass.

Pan-fried bass for breakfast the next day was a real Missouri tradition I brought back to Massachusetts with me. We'd also catch and eat bluegill or sunfish, something New Englanders refer to as "kivers" (pronounced *kih-vuzz* in a New England accent). This is a vile fish by Yankee table standards.

I learned to be accurate with a .410 shotgun and a .22 caliber rifle before the age of ten. Both frogs' legs and squirrel make fine dishes. Neither one tastes like chicken though. In my experience, only chickens taste like chicken!

My granddad's real estate dealings supplemented his coal mining career. Miner safety was not of much concern back then. He had my dad and his brothers working in a mine one day. As Granddad rested outside the mine, the Lord imparted upon him to get his sons out of there! Granddad called to his boys, and just as they exited the shaft, the mine collapsed completely!

Granddad was afflicted with both black lung and emphysema as a result of his extensive coal mining. He would eventually die from the associated health complications. A Massachusetts lawyer in this day and age would have had a field day.

He was a hard man on my dad and his brothers, but he was very gentle on me. Most summers, he and my grand mom, Lola Mae, would spend a month or so with us in Massachusetts. Since my dad worked some 70 hours a week at his dealership, Granddad and I would spend our days hunting everything from edible mushrooms to bullfrogs. He would labor with his breathing problems in the New England humidity, but was always eager for an adventure with me. We did a fair amount of fishing too. The largemouth were more scarce, but the kivers abundant. Pan fried blue-gill breakfasts had become popular in my mom's kitchen too—a tradition I have passed on to my son and daughter.

Granddad was born decades after the Civil War ended, but his grandfather, Julius Ragsdale, Sr., lived through the border state raids as a child and downloaded his strong frontier beliefs onto him. Granddad carried those rugged 19th Century ideals into our conversations and my childhood lessons. Granddad died while I was in college. I miss his presence and influence on my life.

My grand mom was the quintessential frontier homestead wife. Smoking meats and canning all sorts of fruits and vegetables during the growing season for use as family sustenance occupied a majority of her time. Her humble rural beginnings included a father who smoked a corn cob pipe and a mother who enjoyed chewing plug tobacco. I remember meeting them as a very small child.

My mom's side of the family came from equally humble beginnings, including farming in West Boylston, Massachusetts and transporting the produce daily onto Shrewsbury Street, an Italian-American residential neighborhood in the city of Worcester. My great grandfather would bring his load by horse-drawn cart some twenty miles round trip each day. Because the East was settled so much earlier than the Midwest, my Mother's father, Louis DiPasquale, was the last generation to farm in Massachusetts.

Grampy worked his grandfather's farm every summer during the early years of his life. As a youngster, he later sold newspapers on Main Street in Worcester despite his father's embarrassment at the indignity of his son hocking papers on a street corner. He pressed grapes in the basement for his father's wine and earned a whopping 10 cents a day at a local bakery. When his father Antonio (a first generation Italian immigrant) died at a very young age, Grampy quit school to work and feed his mother and three siblings.

He married his sweetheart Ruth (who despite great intellectual promise had also quit school to feed her family) and went into military service during World War II, despite the couple expecting their first baby—my mom. Having missed her birth, he was granted a short leave to see my newborn mom's face at a train station by match-light. They named her Beverly Ruth.

After the war and discharge from the U.S. Army—and with no formal education—Grampy worked his way to General Manager and Vice President of a major national plastics company having plants in Central Massachusetts. He is my only living Grandparent. He lost my Grandmother to Alzheimer's several years ago.

At 91 years young he still lives alone in his own lakefront condominium and has the best attitude of anyone I remember knowing in my life (along with my wife Lauri). I have hours of taped interviews on his life experiences, that will serve as a book in and of itself one day. He is strong, courageous and draws the attention of beautiful widows all over Worcester. Nonetheless, he is fiercely loyal and refuses to breach his marriage covenant to my grandmother—which he holds in life *and* in death—to this day!

After the war, Grammy worked as a checkout clerk at the local International Grocers Association market. My mom had the responsibility of caring for her younger sister and brother before and after school each day, leaving little time for her personal interests. I understand she was quite a competitive roller skater in those days! Upon graduating high school with honors, she worked at a large insurance company as a telephone operator. She also babysat for the Gilman family. And here is where my mom and dad's stories collide and my service in the car business begins.

My dad's sister had been the first and only member of the Ragsdale clan ever to visit New England. She married and remained in Central Massachusetts. Following his discharge from U.S. Army service, my dad made an agreement with himself to be financially successful—a plan that did not include any of the following: mining, farming, digging fence-post holes for 10 cents apiece, babysitting turkey farms overnight, working as a railroad telegraph operator or anything of this sort. He decided to leave those experiences back in Missouri and see what opportunities a new part of the country had to offer him. He had a place to stay at his sister's and only $365 in his pocket!

Darrell Gilman Sr. was sales manager at a local car dealership. While meeting and falling in love with my future mom, the babysitter, my dad decided to accompany Daryl to work one day. The dealer challenged him into waiting on a customer. Dad accepted the challenge and ended up taking an order and cash payment over the customer's coffee table. Needless to say, Dad was hired by that dealer on the spot! Dad's life, Mom's life, and the future lives of my sisters and me went from agriculture to retail just that fast.

Dad earned some $22,000 during his first year in the car business, compared to average non-industry wages at $4,500. My dad fulfilled his promise of financial success to himself and would only return to Missouri to visit family and expose me and my sisters to the rural upbringing he left behind.

He married Mom in 1964 while working as a sales manager for that same dealer. My Mom quit her telephone operator job when I was born in 1966. Dad later found a piece of property West of Boston, took on an auto mechanic for a partner, and started his own used car business. In 1972 he found a rural Chevrolet dealership for sale in Spencer, Massachusetts. The place was basically a pile of parts and a few shop lifts in a converted old dairy barn. But he could stretch and buy it, so he did.

I remember hanging Chevrolet point of purchase posters up in the showroom windows with him and the elation he showed when a female motorist driving by gave a curious look towards the building. "Did you see her look? She looked!" he exclaimed. I worked there every Saturday, as well as every summer from that point on. I swept the shop floors, detailed new and used cars, and picked through the wholesale clunkers for loose change and lost "treasures."

I graduated to minor shop duties, such as changing oil and tires, running the wheel-balancer machine, turning brake rotors on a lathe, and when I got my driver's license, running for parts. I would run mostly to Chevy dealers for parts, as the proliferation of parts "Jobbers" hadn't yet manifested in 1982. In the summer of 1984, Dad put me through a sales training school sponsored by General Motors back when they had a training facility in Dedham, Massachusetts.

In 1988, I graduated with a BA in Journalism (minor in Sociology/ Religious Studies) from The University of Massachusetts, Amherst. I began with my father full-time at the dealership upon graduation, including 10 weeks away at dealer school classes. I graduated from both the NADA Dealer Candidate Academy and Chevrolet Dealership Management School in 1989.

By 1991 I convinced my father and a potential partner to purchase a defunct Pontiac-Cadillac dealership in Worcester, Massachusetts. I would receive no ownership interest in the company, but I was charged with running it for the partners. My Pontiac DM introduced me to a stunning young lady named Lauri Avolizi, also a Pontiac DM, but operating a dealership territory from Massachusetts up to the Canadian border. We dated on the sly for six months before she resigned from General Motors so we could become engaged. Seven months later we married. Lauri worked in the business with me 50 to 60 hours per week opening and operating stores for five years before we began having children.

In 1996, two years before Wyatt, our first child was born, I purchased the majority share of the Pontiac-Cadillac store, which satisfied a personal goal of becoming a franchised dealer before the age of 30. In 1997 I culminated fourteen months of negotiations with a bankruptcy court to purchase a four-acre tract of land and a 22,000 square foot facility from the defunct Fretter Corporation. The acquisition was to be made on behalf of my father and operated as a "one-price, no-negotiations, Used Car Superstore." I received a forty percent share of the operating company but no interest in the real estate. Lauri was due with Wyatt in four short months. Nonetheless, she was still at it, opening the store with me while carrying our son into his third trimester. In 1998 Kia Motors America (KMA) awarded me a franchise for the new location and our first child was born.

In 2000 I opened three Indian Motorcycle dealerships, one co-located at the Shrewsbury Kia dealership, another in Boston, and a third in Myrtle Beach, South Carolina. The Myrtle Beach dealership required a full month of renovations, which I attended to personally. Lauri watched our then two-year-old Wyatt, while carrying our second child, Isabella, into her third trimester. The next two years would be filled with almost as much traveling as I had done in 1989 with the two dealer schools. Except unlike in 1989, I was married with one child and another on the way.

I soon had contracts to open Indian dealerships in Hartford, Connecticut; Springfield, Massachusetts; Atlanta, Georgia; and Raleigh, North Carolina. However, I changed my plans when Indian's unsold inventory was building up at the factory, and they became slow at paying warranty claims and rebate reimbursements. In 2003 I sold my contracts and locations to more optimistic operators. Within a year, Indian Motorcycle of Gilroy, California, folded in bankruptcy.

In 2002 I purchased my father's remaining interest in the Chevrolet, Pontiac-Cadillac and Kia stores, as well as two pieces of dealership real estate for $5.85 million. My mortgage payments totaled $63,000 per month before taxes or insurance—a big bite for a 36-year-old. In February 2004 I constructed and opened an additional Kia store just 11 miles away from the Shrewsbury Kia store due to factory pressure. Of course, just four months later, Kia changed their dealer incentive program, reducing per unit compensation from $1,800 to $350 per car. Their untimely shift put both stores into six-figure monthly losses. My companies went from fueling growth through profits to losing millions. Kia did not care.

Later that year, I opened a 35,000-square-foot Honda facility that had been approved and awarded to me as an "open-point" a decade earlier. At the time of the appointment, I was the youngest ever in the history of Honda. I may still hold that record, but I am unsure. For ten years, my father and I carried 20 acres of vacant property in anticipation of the opening, while Honda slugged it out with abutting dealers over territorial disputes.

In 2005 I sold my Pontiac-Cadillac dealership. In 2006 I sold my Honda dealership. In 2007 I added a Kia franchise next door to my Chevrolet dealership in order to try and replace the sagging domestic truck market. The store went from making $1.4 million per year to losing $100,000 per month. It didn't work. In 2008 I sold Chevrolet back to GM and the newest Kia store next to door to my father. The original Kia dealership was sold to yet another party.

I am happy to be out of the day-to-day grind so many of my friends still endure. I am grateful to God for the timing of my business sales and exit, especially before all the turbulent economic poop hit the fan. In most of my childhood and all my adult life, I worked in this industry, learning a few important lessons. You can never count on an automaker or their programs beyond tomorrow. You can never count on banks being there for you beyond today. As a car dealer, you are on your own, fortunate to have a handful of trusted friends, reliable employees, and a supportive family.

Thanks again for reading my book. If you enjoyed it, please tell your friends. More information is available to you at either www.CarDealerLife.com or www.MarkRagsdale.com. If you wish to make personal contact with me, email CarWreck@MarkRagsdale.com. Be sure to put "READ CAR WRECK" in the subject line and include your best daytime and evening phone number so I can contact you.

ENDNOTES

1. Trademarked language learning software, Rosetta Stone Ltd., www.rosettastone.com

2. Grant Cardone, "Sales Training Guide," Orlando, FL., 1997, http://marketingyes.com/initial_meeting.htm, http://marketingyes.com/grant_cardone.htm.

3. Customer Support: Edmunds.com, www.edmunds.com , (accessed February 4, 2009).

4. Answers.yahoo.com, "Resolved question, 2008," http://answers.yahoo.com/question/index?qid=20071107155202AAsM6qB, (accessed March 3, 2009).

5. David Kiley, "Toyota's Lexus leads quality survey," *USA Today*, http://www.usatoday.com/money/autos/2001-05-17-jdpower.htm, (accessed March 30, 2009).

6. J.D. Power and Associates Reports, Vehicle Dependability Study, "Deterioration in Vehicle Quality During the First Three Years of Ownership Has a Major Impact on Customer Satisfaction and Advocacy, August 7, 2008" http://www,.theautochannel.com/news/2008/08/07/095711.html, (accessed March 30, 2009).

7. "The Rule of 78s," http://en.wikipedia.org/wiki/Rule_of_78s, (accessed March 10, 2009)

8. Morris A. Nunes, "Rule of 78s, How it Works," © 2001, Pine Grove Software, Princeton, NJ. All rights reserved, © 2001, Morris A. Nunes. All rights reserved., http://www.pine-grove.com/reading%20room/rule-of-78s.htm, (accessed March 4, 2009).

9. Jennifer Reed, Auto Group Editor, "PIN: Average down-paymentJumps Along with Age of Trade-Ins," September. 30 2008, http://www.subprimenews.com/spn/news/story.html?id=798, (accessed February 14, 2009)

10. Bureau of Labor Statistics, CPI data, "History of new car costs and average inflation," November 11, 2008, http://freeby50.blogspot.com/2008/11/history-of-new-car-costs-and-average.html, (accessed Feb 18, 2009)

11. Rosland B. Gammon, "Dealers hunt upside-down buyers with leases, incentives and long-term loans," *Automotive News* (May 5, 2008).: p38

12. David Shenk, "Data Smog: Surviving the Information Glut, 1997," http://74.125.47.132/search?q=cache:J15DAWagxe8J:www.storyofstuff.com/pdfs/annie_leonard_facts.pdf+average+american+sees+OR+views+OR+hears+advertising+OR+ads+OR+advertisements+per+day+15,000&cd=1&hl=en&ct=clnk&gl=us, (accessed Feb 25, 2009).

13. Michael Brower and Warren Leon, "Practical Advice from the Union of Concerned Scientists," http://www.ucsusa.org/publications/guide.ch1.html, (accessed Mar 4 2009.)

14. "Nada data," *AutoExec,* May 2000, http://www.nada.org/NR/rdonlyres/0FE75B2C-69F0-4039-89FE-1366B5B86C97/0/NADAData08_no.pdf, (accessed March 31, 2009).

15. Bureau of Labor Statistics, "Career Guide to Industries: Automobile Dealers," http://www.bls.gov/oco/cg/cgs025.htm#emply, (accessed March 25, 2009).

16. "Nada data," AutoExec May 2008, http://www.nada.org/NR/rdonlyres/0FE75B2C-69F0-4039-89FE-1366B5B86C97/0/NADAData08_no.pdf, (accessed March 31, 2009).

17. Ibid.

18. Newt Gingrich, "Suspend Mark-to Market Now!" *Forbes,* (September 29, 2008), http://www.forbes.com/2008/09/29/mark-to-market-oped-cx_ng_0929gingrich.html, (accessed March 20, 2009).

19. Ibid.

20. "UAW applauds auto loans, but says workers must not be singled out for unfair conditions, December 19, 2008," http://www.uaw.org/auto/12_19_08auto1.cfm, (accessed March 3, 2009).

21. "Encyclopedia:UAW," http://www.nationmaster.com/encyclopedia/United_Auto_Workers, (accessed March 12, 2009).

22. Chris Isadore, "73,000 workers walk in nationwide GM strike, September 24th, 2007," http://money.cnn.com/2007/09/24/news/companies/gm_uaw_strikedeadline/?postversion, (accessed March 19, 2009).

23. "Contract Protects UAW Jobs: UAW NewsGram," *New York Times,* (October 2007), http://www.nytimes.com/packages/pdf/business/20071015_CHRYSLER.pdf, (accessed March 15 2009).

24. Shel Silverstein, *Giving Tree,* (New York: HarperCollins, 1964).

25. "Nada data," *AutoExec,* May 2008,, http://www.nada.org/NR/rdonlyres/0FE75B2C-69F0-4039-89FE-1366B5B86C97/0/NADAData08_no.pdf, (accessed March 3, 2009).

26. "Obama orders more fuel-efficient cars by 2011," *Auto Industry News,* http://automarketworld.wordpress.com, (accessed March 20, 2009).

INDEX

Abraham, Lisa, 194
accountability, lack of, 122, 124
accounting rules, 146–149, 153, 212
actual cash value (ACV), 45–47, 213
advertising by car dealers, 73–78
   government regulations, 74–75
   loss leaders, 76–77
   payment emphasis, 76, 77–78
   statistics, 73–74
agendas, of customers *versus* car dealers, 3
AIG (American International Group), 189
ALG (Automotive Lease Guide), 69, 206–207
Alick, Barry, 124
Allison-Fisher Purchase Funnel, 71
American International Group (AIG), 189
appraisals, trade-in, 48–49
Asian imports, 186–187, 188
asset-backed securities, 150–153
audits of dealers by automakers, 101–106, 201–202
auto loans
   12-month, 33
   36-month, 59–60
   42-month, 59–60, 206
   60-month, 34
   amount, 82
   banks, 141–142, 149–150
   dealer financing, 77
   debt on applications, 83
   financing basics for consumers, 212–213
   income on applications, 80–81, 83

increasing length of, 37
increasing payments of, 36–37
negative equity and, 82
Rule of 78s, 31–35, 38–39
shorter-term, 214
structuring applications for approval, 81–83
automakers
   access to dealer bank accounts, 104–105, 142–143
   accountability, lack of, 122, 124
   audits of dealers by, 101–106, 201–202
   corrective actions for, 199–206
   dealer network manipulation, 115
   dealer profitability and, 200–201
   dealer reimbursement procedures, 100–101
   district managers, 116, 121–122, 123–124, 207
   factory middle-management, 122
   federal loans to, 155–156, 158–160
   immunity, 122
   incentive programs, 53–55, 202–203, 224
   leasing, 69–71
   production control, 203
   relationship with dealers, 99–108, 115–124
   rental companies/fleet sales, 27–29, 204
   repair restrictions on dealers by, 105, 106–107
   training for dealers, 116–119
   zone managers, 116, 122, 207

automobile franchise system, 87–97
benefits of, 90–91
fast food franchise system compared
to, 87–89, 90–91
megadealers, 93–94
money made by dealers, 94–96
need for dealers, 96–97
termination of dealers, 49, 91–92,
96–97, 163–166
types of dealers, 92–93
automobile technicians, 109–113
Automotive Lease Guide (ALG), 69,
206–207
Avolizi, Mary Ann, 193
Avolizi, Robert, 193

Baker, Robert, 126, 194
balloon-note financing, 67, 216
bankruptcy, 27–28, 93, 156–158, 159
banks
auto loans, 141–142, 149–150
floorplan financing, 137–144
leasing, 68–69
mark-to-market rule of accounting
and, 146–149
mortgages, 138–140, 141, 146–149
"no-excuses" risk management, 180
Bell, Scott, 124
Bernard, Paul, 194
Berquist, Gloria, 171
Blevins, Owen, 194
BMW, 161
bondholders, 138–140, 156–157, 158,
159
Bouvier, Brenda, 194
Buckley, Regis, 124
Bush, George W., 155–156, 158
Bush, Terry, 194
Business Development Centers, 117
business managers, 84–85, 128–130

Cadillac Sedan Deville, 21, 70–71
CAFE (Corporate Average Fuel
Economy) standards, 169–171
Call-Rooms, 117
cap-cost reductions, 61, 63–64
car dealer employees, 125–136
bad, 128–133
continuous improvement teams,
208
good, 126–128
selecting, 208–209
ugly, 133–136

car dealers. *See also* advertising by car
dealers
advertising, 73–78
agenda, 3
audits by automakers, 101–106,
201–202
automaker access to dealer bank
accounts, 104–105, 142–143
automaker reimbursement
procedures, 100–101
business managers, 84–85, 128–130
corrective actions for, 206–209
dealing with financial challenges of
customers, 9–10
expenses, annual, 95
financing through, 77
gathering information from
customers, 7–8
incentive programs, 53–55,
202–203, 224
loan application structuring for
approval, 81–83
maintaining choice of, 48–49
megadealers, 93–94
money made by, 94–96
monthly meetings, 6
need for, 96–97
net profit, 94, 95
network manipulation by
automakers, 115
profitability and automakers,
200–201
recession's effect on sales, 95–96
relationship with automakers,
99–108, 115–124
repair restrictions by automakers,
105, 106–107
sales, annual, 95
service departments, 109–113
statistics, 91–92, 94–95
termination of, 49, 91–92, 96–97,
163–166
trade-ins, 41–49
training by automakers, 116–119
training by dealers, 5–6, 119–120
types, 92–93
under water, 21–22
Card Check, 162–163, 186
Cardone, Grant (Cardone Enterprises),
5, 10, 194
Carr, Michael, 123
cash, paying, 59
cash down payment in leasing, 61, 63–64

O'Neill, Steve, 194
Oracle software, 176
oversight, 181

Paldino, Pete, 194
Palmer, Garry, 105
Paparella, Don, 123
Patrick, Deval, 174
Pelosi, Nancy, 28
pencils
    discount, 46
    initial, 42
    second, 79–80
    trade allowance, 46
Penttila, Dave, 195
Penttila, Pam, 195
Perry, Charlie (C. Perry and Associates),
    194
Pontiac, 94, 123–124. See also General
    Motors
Pontiac-Cadillac dealers, 104–105
Power, J.D., 17–18
preferred shareholders, 157
Press, Langdon Street, 194
principal, 31
profit
    dealer, 94, 95, 200–201
    gross margins on service, 111–112
    Make the Most Net Profit game,
    118
    net, 94, 95
proof of income waivers, 81

quality, initial, 16–18
Qutab, Abbas M.D.(Elan Vital), 194
Qutab, Mitz, 194

Ragsdale, Beverly, 193, 221
Ragsdale, George, 217–219, 221–223,
    224
Ragsdale, Isabella, 193, 224, 237
Ragsdale, Lauri Avolizi, 124, 131–132,
    193,223, 224
Ragsdale, Lola Mae, 219, 220
Ragsdale, Mark,
    About the author, 237
    influences on, 217–225
Ragsdale Motor Group, 194
Ragsdale, Otis, 217–218, 219–220
Ragsdale, Wyatt, 193, 223-224, 237
Ragsdale-Fuller Pontiac Cadillac, 128
Ragsdale Pontiac Cadillac, 164–165
Rattner, Steven, 166

rebates
    audits by automaker, 101–102
    described, 19–23
    fronted by dealers, 100
    replacing with upside-down aid for
    consumers, 204–206
recession, effect on dealer new vehicle
    sales, 95–96
Recore, Bob, 194
Reed, Glen, 194
references for job applicants, 128–129,
    130
Reidy, Bob, 51–52
rental company/fleet sales, 23–29
    depreciation and, 24–25
    initial sales to rental car companies,
    23
    negative equity and, 25–26
    reducing or eliminating, 204
    repurchase from rental car
    companies, 23–26
    switching vehicles and, 85–86
    why automakers play fleet games,
    27–29
rental fees, GM warranty audit of, 103
repair restrictions, on dealers by
    automakers, 105, 106–107
repeat repair attempts, GM warranty
    audit of, 103
resale values
    Honda, 26–27, 204
    Toyota, 26–27
Reynolds, Barbara, 194
right of first refusal, in franchise
    agreements, 89
risk management,"no-excuses," 180
Roving Sage salespeople, 132–133, 209
Rossetti, Robert (Northeast Seminars),
    194
Royal Bank of Scotland, 138, 140
Rule of 78s, 31–35, 38–39

sales, annual dealer, 95
sales managers, 4
salespeople
    compensation plans, 130–131,
    132–133
    Roving Sage, 132–133, 209
Sanders, Robin, 123–124
Saturn, 164
second pencil, 79–80
Securities and Exchange Commission
    (SEC), 146

ABOUT THE AUTHOR

author photo by Romona M. Preston

As a former car dealer from a car dealer family, Mark brings 25 years of experience to his insightful new book, *Car Wreck*. Passionate and articulate, he enthusiastically lays out the "fixes" for the car industry, which is currently hammered by decades of accumulated finance abuses, unholy political motivations, and unadulterated greed.

After earning a journalism degree from the University of Massachusetts in 1988, Mark graduated from both industry and manufacturer-sponsored car dealer schools. In 1989 he rejoined his father's Chevrolet dealership, where he had dedicated his Saturdays and summers from the age of seven. By age 24, he ran a Pontiac-Cadillac dealership on behalf of his father and a partner. By 30, he purchased the majority share of the store. Over the next twelve years, he proceeded to purchase or construct five additional franchised automobile dealerships and three motorcycle stores. He has represented Chevrolet, Pontiac, Cadillac, Kia, Honda, Excelsior-Henderson, and Indian Motorcycle.

His experience in the industry is broad. He has served on the Kia National Dealer Council, as Chairman of a National Automobile Dealers Association (NADA) 20-Group, as Director of the Massachusetts State Automobile Dealers Association, and as President and/or Director for several different dealer marketing associations.

In 2008 Ragsdale sold his dealerships. He now writes and consults with car dealers, policy makers, and other industry professionals. He resides in Shrewsbury, Massachusetts, with his beautiful wife, Lauri, and their two children, Wyatt and Isabella.